COUNTERTRANSFERENCE ENACTMENT

**How Institutions
and Therapists
Actualize Primitive
Internal Worlds**

Richard Shur, Ph.D.

JASON ARONSON INC.
*Northvale, New Jersey
London*

Production Editor: Judith D. Cohen

This book was set in 11 point Garamond by Lind Graphics of Upper Saddle River, New Jersey, and printed and bound by Haddon Craftsmen of Scranton, Pennsylvania.

Library of Congress Cataloging-in-Publication Data

Shur, Richard.
    Countertransference enactment : How institutions and therapists
actualize primitive internal worlds / by Richard Shur.
        p. cm.
    Includes bibliographical references and index.
    ISBN 1-56821-098-1
    1. Countertransference (Psychology) 2. Psychiatric hospitals—
Sociological aspects. 3. Psychiatric hospitals—Employees—
Psychology. 4. Mental health personnel—Psychology. 5. Defense
mechanisms (Psychology) I. Title.
    [DNLM: 1. Countertransference (Psychology) 2. Object Attachment.
3. Hospitals, Psychiatric. 4. Medical Staff, Hospital—psychology.
WM 62 S562c 1994]
    RC489.C68S57   1994
616.89′14—dc20
DNLM/DLC
for Library of Congress   93-11932

Manufactured in the United States of America. Jason Aronson Inc. offers books and cassettes. For information and catalog write to Jason Aronson Inc., 230 Livingston Street, Northvale, New Jersey 07647.

Dedicated to the patients and staff
of 6A-North

Contents

Acknowledgment

I would like to thank L. Bryce Boyer, M.D., and Peter Giovacchini, M.D., who graciously took time out of their very busy schedules to read an early version of my manuscript, and who offered encouragement and helpful suggestions at a time when I was sorely in need of both. More recently, Dr. Giovacchini agreed—much to my delight—to contribute a chapter of his own. Entitled "Collective Countertransference and Parallel Process," his essay expands the discussion of primitive enactment into areas I had not been able to capture in my own clinical material.

Ann-Louise Silver, M.D., was equally kind. Her very detailed and astute critique of portions of the manuscript helped me gain a better understanding of a number of thorny problems. Much of the book's organization and approach to its topic have been influenced by her comments.

Closer to home, I have been fortunate to have the advice and counsel of Kevin Keenan, Ph.D., and Etta Saxe, Ph.D. Since my clinical internship, when Dr. Saxe was one of my teachers, I have valued her ability to define and get to the heart of complicated issues. She applied that talent to her reading of my manuscript, and I am certain it is the better for it. Dr. Keenan's detailed comments on the text have also been invaluable, particularly in helping me think more clearly about my prospective readers and how to present the material in a manner that addresses their needs and circumstances.

I would also like to thank the many clinical supervisors, consultants, colleagues, and students who have worked with me over the years, especially Patrick Kavanaugh, Ph.D., and Xavier Burgoyne, M.D. In their very different ways, these two gifted clinicians helped me build the foundation on which this book was constructed.

My sister, Marsha Isard, kindly gave me the benefit of her editorial experience. Her sound advice and interesting observations were, as always, very helpful.

Finally, I would like to thank my wife, Beverley Francis Shur, and my sons, Michael and Marc. Without their patience, encouragement, and understanding, none of this would have been possible.

It is one sort of observation that some gynaecologists seem to have a need to perform hysterectomies on the merest excuse; it is another that some women seem to seek hysterectomy on the merest excuse. It is not easy to say . . . which of these is the victim of each other's wishes, which has the more significant ailment, and which derives more comfort from the treatment. In a human relationship the study of one person, no matter which one, is likely to throw light on the behaviour of the other.

T. F. Main

Introduction

This book grew out of my fourteen years of work with severely disturbed patients in psychiatric hospitals. Its purpose is to examine how certain commonly accepted hospital practices, procedures, and structures support potentially injurious forms of countertransference enactment. Because they help to disguise, ward off, or discharge tensions within the staff, countertransference structures play a crucial role in the hospital's psychological equilibrium. It is my hope that this book will contribute to a more accurate understanding of their function in the treatment milieu and of the powerful undercurrents of feeling and fantasy they are bound up with.

Psychoanalytic investigation makes it impossible to regard the existence of countertransference-enhancing structures simply as isolated errors in hospital or ward practice. Psychiatric hospitals operate on two contradictory but interrelated levels: in addition to the manifest mission of providing treatment, they deploy an array of procedures, organizational arrangements, and modes of thinking and acting that support tendencies in the staff to enact or distance itself from the anxieties and impulses evoked by severely disturbed patients.

An institutional arrangement functions as a countertransference structure if it facilitates countertransference enactment and/or defense. In the pages that follow, I will be examining a range of hospital procedures. Many of these seemingly quite unremarkable practices unconsciously support regressed modes of functioning, in particular the projection, enactment, and reintrojection of primitive internalized object relations.

Effective hospital treatment of severely regressed patients is dependent on the ability of staff members to contain and psychologically process the highly disturbing emotions, impulses, and anxieties evoked in the course of the work. Entrenched countertransference-supporting structures disrupt this process; they shield the staff at the cost of perpetuating mental and emotional dysfunction. Containment is difficult under the best of circumstances. It is much less likely to occur when the staff is provided with a virtual menu of institutionally sanctioned procedures that support reflexive enactment and/or disengagement. Yet, because of their efficacy in allaying primitive anxieties, countertherapeutic institutional arrangements are usually highly defended and resistant to examination and modification.

In this book, I reflect on encounters with patients, staff, and hospital bureaucracies in settings where accepted procedures supported miscarriages of treatment. My critique is sometimes harsh. I have struggled to temper it by continually reminding myself and the reader that countertransference structures are valued and defended because they help sustain a tolerable balance under conditions of emotional threat that are difficult for outsiders to imagine. I hope that this knowledge has helped me bring some greater degree of equanimity to my topic.

Chapter 1 consists of an introduction to the concept of countertransference structure. In particular, I focus on structures that facilitate the enactment of dehumanization, splitting, and omnipotence. These three impulse/defense constellations—sometimes in pure culture but more often in combination—play a crucial and unique role in the staff's attempt to cope with primitive tensions. Thus, Chapter 1 forms the foundation for understanding the vicissitudes of transference/countertransference enactment in the settings described here.

Chapters 2 and 3 focus on psychiatry and nursing, the two key practitioner groups in inpatient settings. From this vantage point, the ward's organization; its distribution of authority, responsibility, and status; its division of labor; its treatment ideology; and certain of its interpersonal/interdisciplinary arrangements are examined. The purpose is to point out how each of these factors may play a surprisingly potent but usually unseen role in perpetuating primitive transference/countertransference equilibria.

Chapter 4 describes how the interdisciplinary treatment team—under optimal conditions—can function as a sort of containment receptacle into which projective identifications are funneled and clinically processed, thus interrupting the cycle of reflexive defense and enactment. It also examines institutional and countertransference factors that enhance or block team functions. This chapter provides some hint of the potential capacity of milieu treatment to gain access to and make use of the potent psychological tensions that pervade wards where disturbed patients are treated.

Chapter 5 focuses on the treatment alliance as a potentially humanizing influence in the all too readily dehumanized milieu of the psychiatric hospital. The discussion is intended to demonstrate how the staff's commitment to an alliance enhances the person-to-person quality of working with primitive patients. In contrast, unilateral conceptions of treatment are seen as facilitating and disguising aggression-infiltrated interactions and attitudes.

Chapter 6 consists of an examination of the clinical impact of the hospital bureaucracy. First, case material is provided showing how centralized administrative structures and inter-disciplinary turf battles can add to the propensity for splitting, resentment, and devaluation on the wards. Additional material illustrates the obsession with control, surveillance, and coercion encountered among bureaucrats at certain hospitals. The purpose of this chapter is to show how mistrustful, punitive, and power-oriented administrative methods and attitudes eventually permeate the wards, contributing to a climate in which patients' grandiose and persecutory fantasies receive repeated and constant confirmation in reality.

In Chapter 7, Dr. Peter Giovacchini addresses and enlarges upon a number of the issues raised in earlier sections. He emphasizes the disparity between the self experience of therapist and primitive patient and the resulting disruption in the therapist's equilibrium when a radically ego-dystonic component of the patient has been introjected. This formulation adds to our ability to appreciate the vulnerability of therapists and other hospital staff. The dysfunctional defenses discussed throughout this book are deeply ingrained precisely because the disruption the staff is exposed to is of daunting proportions.

Dr. Giovacchini is also interested in the parallel processes that develop when the psychopathology of patient and therapist dovetail, and he provides provocative clinical material suggesting the potential complexity of these interrelationships. He notes, for example, that when components of the self-representation of therapist and patient are similar, it is easier for fusions to occur manifested by unconscious collusion and shared enactments. The behavioral or interpersonal dimension of the enactment can be more adequately understood in relation to corresponding intrapsychic structures and representations.

I would particularly like to call attention to Dr. Giovacchini's discussion of the loss of an intrapsychic treatment focus. In my chapters, I have emphasized the propensity of symptom-oriented methods to degenerate into dehumanizing behavior control and the enactment of countertransference aggression. Dr. Giovacchini adds the very important and interesting observation that the staff too becomes dehumanized when patients are experienced and conceptualized as part-objects who lack an inner world.

This book is organized around case studies. Since I am surveying a wide variety of hospital practices, the presentations are, of necessity, incomplete and focused primarily on those aspects that most directly pertain to the processes under discussion. I hope that clinicians will compare these observations and formulations to their own experience and find in them some measure of validity and usefulness.

The cases are drawn from my clinical experience and that of students or colleagues, acquired at a variety of state and private psychiatric hospitals. Identifying information is disguised to protect the privacy of patients and staff members. However, it has not been possible to avoid identifying the administrative position or professional affiliation of certain staff members.

Freud (1912) very early recognized that unconscious processes are communicated to the analyst through the receptivity of his own unconscious. This receptivity carries the potential for destructiveness as well as for growth and development. It is my hope that the clinical discussions in this book will partially illuminate this inherent tension.

Countertransference Structures

COUNTERTRANSFERENCE AS COMMUNICATION

In the classical psychoanalytic view (Greenson 1967, Reich 1951, 1960), countertransference refers to the therapist's sustained or episodic transference to a patient in which the patient is unconsciously experienced as someone from the therapist's past. This formulation emphasizes how the therapist's intrapsychic distortions interfere with an ability to accurately understand and/or respond to the patient's transference.

The classical view can be traced back to Freud's attempt (1910) to take account of a disturbing phenomenon that he probably first became aware of while pondering Breuer's treatment of Anna O. Freud characterized unconscious feelings toward the patient—such as those experienced and enacted by Breuer—as a countertransference, growing out of the analyst's own complexes and resistances. These feelings constituted an impediment to treatment that had to be overcome by self-analysis.

However, Freud was not unaware of the communicative dimension of the countertransference. In 1912, he described the analyst's unconscious as "a receptive organ" that must be turned "to the transmitting unconscious of the patient. . . . [The] doctor's unconscious is able, from the derivatives of the unconscious which are communicated to him, to reconstruct the unconscious, which has determined the patient's free associations" (pp. 111–112).

It is, of course, noteworthy that the earlier formulation became the classical one. It took many years for the implications of Freud's second statement to be widely accepted and enlarged upon. Probably, there are few clearer illustrations of the impact of anxiety on psychoanalytic exploration.

Inherent in the notion of countertransference as communicative is that it can facilitate therapy by providing access to deeper layers of the patient's inner world. Heimann's important paper (1950) played a key role in bringing this aspect of countertransference analysis into the mainstream of practice.

Fromm-Reichmann, one of the founders of contemporary psychoanalytic work with severely regressed patients, attempted to integrate the communicative and classical approaches. In her text on intensive psychotherapy (1950), she describes experiencing an uncharacteristically intense level of anxiety in reaction to an assaultive patient. Since she usually worked comfortably with dangerous patients, she realized her fear stemmed from her own unconscious processes. In consultation with a supervisor, she was able to understand the negative countertransference and it then subsided. Subsequently, she and the patient were able to resume a constructive therapeutic collaboration.

However, Fromm-Reichmann went beyond the classical view in that she recognized a reciprocal quality in the transference reactions of therapist and patient. She advised therapists to use their personal reactions as an instrument in understanding hidden implications of patients' communication and as a guide in conducting therapy. In reading her clinical material, one is struck by the astuteness with which she gleans crucial psychological insights from interpersonal reactions to patients.

The work of Harold Searles has been of immense importance in sensitizing clinicians to the role of countertransference analysis in the therapy of severely disturbed patients. Although many of his observations and formulations now seem self-evident and indispensable, at the time he published his initial collection of papers (1965), intense primitive reactions in the therapist still tended to be regarded as destructive, inappropriate, and indicative of unresolved pathology.

The richly detailed, frank, and compelling clinical material presented by Searles made it virtually impossible to continue to ignore, minimize, or pathologize primitive countertransferences. Because his work has come to occupy such a central place in our literature, it is easy to forget the personal courage and conviction that must have been required to bring it out.

An emphasis on the patient's contribution to the therapist's experience may be seen clearly in the writings of clinicians who have been influenced by the work of Melanie Klein. Racker (1968), for example, describes cases in which the transference neurosis exists in tandem with a corresponding countertransference neurosis. In some degree, the therapist's feelings and fantasies reflect and are elicited by the patient's conflicts and distortions. The therapist must understand and resolve the countertransference neurosis in order to assist in resolving the patient's neurosis.

According to Racker, the countertransference transmits vital information concerning the patient's internal self and object relations. A *concordant identification* involves an identification with the patient's self-experience as it becomes activated in a specific unconscious transference. Concordant identifications contribute to empathic awareness of patients' self-experience. In contrast, *complementary identification* refers to the therapist's identification with the object component in the unconscious transference. The therapist may live out either or both components in the interpersonal relationship.

Among British object relations theorists, Winnicott has emphasized the centrality of countertransference as a key to understanding the patient's internal state. His comments on hatred (1949) are especially helpful in the treatment of primitive patients, who not infrequently evoke extreme forms of aggression. If not adequately understood and managed, these feelings may transform the treatment into an exercise in veiled acting out by the therapist.

Ogden (1986), who has been influenced both by Melanie Klein and by the British school defines countertransference as the therapist's unconscious identification with a self or object component of the patient's internal world. However, this formulation appears to limit countertransference proper to those interactions in which a communicative process has occurred. The therapist's transference to the patient, involving genetically determined distortions within the therapist, is apparently considered a separate phenomenon.

While the classical perspective neglects the patient's contribution to the therapist's experience, viewing countertransference solely as an unconscious identification with the patient's internal objects may err in the opposite direction, locating the origin of distortions solely in patients. In fact, countertransferences are most usefully conceptualized as an amalgam, deriving potentially from the patient's and the therapist's unconscious processes.

The most influential current writers place countertransference analysis at the center of work with severely disturbed patients. As the degree of pathology deepens, integrating the countertransference becomes increasingly crucial. Giovacchini (1979) notes that analysts often ward off intolerable countertransferences by convincing themselves that their patient is untreatable. In this sense, treatability "depends more on the analyst's psychic integration than the patient's psychopathology" (p. 236).

Giovacchini notes that the therapist's increasing capacity to tolerate primitive countertransferences makes it possible to treat patients who might otherwise have been considered hopeless. The struggle with dystonic and frightening ego states can enlarge the therapist's capacities. By working with deeply regressed patients, we "receive treatment ourselves so that our therapeutic armamentarium and our knowledge of early developmental phases is enriched sufficiently to diminish the list of conditions that are considered to be contraindications to analysis" (p. 236).

As an example, a state hospital therapist, Dr. W., worked for several years with a threatening aggressive borderline man whose whole purpose in life seemed to be to make him feel small, frightened, incompetent, stupid, and bad intentioned. The patient, Mr. L., was raised by a passive mentally ill mother and an extremely abusive and explosive father. His manifest identification was with the bullying and castrating aspects of his father. He treated others, especially the therapist, with withering scorn and intimidation.

The patient's inability to tolerate the passive, frightened, maternal components of his self-experience was almost palpable. On one occasion, it became necessary to meet in Dr. W.'s off-ward office, as the therapy room on the ward was being painted. Mr. L. had an acute paranoid reaction to this seemingly innocuous alteration of their standard routine. The increased closeness and intimacy implied by being in his therapist's private office triggered intense homosexual anxiety, which could only be warded off by going into a destructive rage. Only when everyone on the ward was thoroughly terrified could the patient feel convinced that others and not he himself were weak, needy, passive, and afraid.

In the course of his treatment, Mr. L. repeatedly evoked these split-off and unacknowledged components of his self-experience in the therapist. Dr. W. found himself immobilized by feelings of depression, anxiety, and defeat when he was with him. His mind seemed incapable of functioning. He was unable to understand the patient's associations, unable to respond coherently to his guilt-inducing interrogations or to his endless threats and demands.

To cope therapeutically with Mr. L.'s contempt and sadistic devaluation, it was necessary for the therapist not only to understand the frightened, passive, "feminized" self the patient was projecting into him, but also to come to grips with certain private anxieties that had been reactivated by session after session of being on the receiving end of Mr. L.'s scornful, castrating bullying. This process took many months and went on largely unconsciously. When Dr. W. finally realized that the unrelenting attacks had stirred up unresolved fears and fantasies involving his father, the connection seemed ridiculously obvious and he could hardly believe that it had not occurred to him much earlier.

What had been necessary, however, was that Dr. W. live with his activated feelings for a long while. During this interim period, he was constantly struggling with the temptation to give up completely on Mr. L. or to respond aggressively to his obnoxious attacks. Either of these alternatives would have constituted an identification in overt behavior with a component of the patient's internal object world, either with his devalued, hopeless, suicidal maternal self or with his attacking sadistic father self.

A sustained enactment of either would have validated Mr. L.'s primitive internal world. Living with his own painful feelings made it possible for Dr. W. to eventually understand an important dimension of the patient's pain. When the time was finally ripe, he was able to talk coherently with Mr. L. about what was transpiring, enabling him to slowly move into a new phase of the transference in which he experienced some connectedness with the helpless defeat and depression he had been eliciting and attacking in his therapist.

PROJECTIVE IDENTIFICATION

If countertransference has a communicative dimension, it is necessary to have some notion of how cognitive and emotional information is transmitted and received. My understanding of the process relies heavily on the concept of projective identification.

Ogden (1982) has provided a comprehensive review and clarification of projective identification. He begins by demonstrating that it is a clinical-level concept, derived from "phenomenological references, all of which lie entirely within the realm of observable psychological and interpersonal experience" (p. 9). He then delineates three phases, involving both intrapsychic and interpersonal elements.

In the first phase, a projector fantasizes ridding himself of a split-off component of his internal world, experienced as intolerably threatening to the self or as in danger of being destroyed. He then exerts pressure on an interpersonal recipient, attempting to induce the recipient to feel his unwanted feelings. The projector needs to believe that the self or object component is located inside the recipient. In the last phase, the recipient may partially identify with and enact the projected component.

The powerful undercurrents of feeling evoked by projective identifications can draw individual members of the staff or even the entire milieu into cycles of enactment that validate the primitive object relation in external reality and make it readily available for reintrojection. When primitive self or object components are repeatedly lived out via treatment interventions or other interpersonal transactions, the milieu is transformed into a medium for perpetuating regressive modes of experience. Heimann (1955) describes this cycle of projection and reintrojection as it occurs in paranoid patients. Schafer (1968) provides a comprehensive elucidation of internalization processes, placing introjection in its developmental context.

In the usual language of the psychiatric hospital, the disturbed and disturbing behavioral and psychological manifestations accompanying projective identifications are *symptoms* requiring active *intervention.* Here, they are examined as mechanisms for maintaining homeostasis under conditions of dire threat and vulnerability. The goal of treatment is not to prematurely or aggressively deprive patients of their symptoms, but to work in a collaborative fashion to foster more adaptive ways of coping with regressive tensions.

The task of the staff, the ward, and the mental hospital is to provide a safe and secure holding environment (Winnicott 1945, 1960) in which it becomes possible for recipients of projective identifications to contain the evoked tensions on a psychological level (Bion 1967). Containing primitive projections involves cognitive and emotional work, as illustrated in the case of Mr. L. I refer to this process as "working over" the projection. Containing and working over requires tolerating levels of anxiety and other dysphoric states that tend to be reflexively discharged on wards where enactment predominates.

By containing the primitive anxieties and part-object components projected into the milieu, members of the treatment team implicitly offer a more mature manner of responding to regressive tensions. These capacities then become available for internalization. In this manner, the cycle of projection and reintrojection of primitive contents and mechanisms is interrupted and a growth-inducing process initiated.

Working with patients such as Mr. L. teaches the therapist extremely valuable but hard-won lessons. Deeply disturbed patients activate our most painful fears and evoke disturbingly empathic resonances. Patients such as Mr. L. bombard us with symptoms that potently move us to react, that seem to cry out for control or retribution or distancing. Symptom tolerance, containment, and working over as required by transference/ countertransference analysis is inherently emotionally demanding. In addition, it is an approach based on a body of theory, clinical skills, and personal experiences that is not easily acquired. Because of these myriad difficulties, wards and hospitals where countertransference enactment pervades treatment may represent the rule rather than the exception.

STUDIES OF THE MILIEU

My thoughts and observations on the treatment milieu have been greatly influenced by the work of Stanton and Schwartz. Their richly detailed examination of Chestnut Lodge, a highly regarded psychiatric hospital in Maryland, uncovered numerous seemingly extraneous institutional factors that were exerting an unsuspected influence on interpersonal relations and psychopathology. I am also indebted to T. F. Main, whose astute observations and analysis helped me think about the powerful regressive pull exerted on staff members by disturbed patients. Kernberg's emphasis on the role of primitive defenses—especially projective identification and splitting—in the evocation and enactment of countertransference reactions has also been essential to my understanding of the milieu.

Stanton and Schwartz (1954) hypothesized that certain regressive "symptoms" could be understood in part as reactions to social and institutional dysfunction. When these were corrected, disturbed behavior often diminished in severity. Their examination of the mental hospital as a complex social structure made it possible to begin to discern the massive but often shadowy influence of institutional practices on behavior, attitudes, relationships, and treatment processes.

The strength of Stanton and Schwartz's approach is its exhaustiveness and its attention to details and connections that others had failed to notice or had dismissed as having little or no clinical impact. However, their reliance on sociological methods and formulations creates certain misleading impressions. Chief among these is the seeming portrayal, in many passages, of mental patients as passive victims of the hospital environment that impinges on them.

For example, in their chapter "Morale and its Breakdown," the authors examine an episode of disintegrative behavior that swept through Chestnut Lodge after certain disruptive administrative changes were effected. I am not aware of another portrayal of the institutional dimension of splitting that compares in thoroughness and complexity. Stanton and Schwartz sift through administrative and social processes in a manner that can only be described as brilliant. However, their method does not permit them to recognize sufficiently that splitting works in two directions. Patients not only react to fault lines in the institution, they actively foster and make use of them, thus actualizing primitive internal part-object relations.

A closely related difficulty is that the writers appear to believe that hospital dynamics can be understood primarily in terms of conscious rational processes. In examining distorted communication among staff and patients, they state that "misunderstandings are *always* [my emphasis] marked by the absence of pertinent information. Supplying the missing information interrupts the misunderstanding or leads to significant alteration in it" (p. 226).

This formulation includes delusional misunderstandings. It gives the impression that psychotic patients fail to operate along rational lines largely because they lack factual information. It also does little justice to the misunderstandings of staff members caught in the grip of powerful irrational emotions.

In their examination of clinical decision-making, Stanton and Schwartz criticize those who attempt to understand clinical decisions "as if the important thing were not what the person in power decides . . . but on the contrary, what sort of person he is" (p. 256). The authors are reacting to an apparent tendency at Chestnut Lodge to undervalue the real content of decisions and interventions. But in trying to correct an imbalance, they have tipped the scales too far in the opposite direction. One gathers that the decision-maker's motivation is only of interest to those who oppose him and who require an ad hominem argument to justify their opposition. This notion is consistent with Stanton and Schwartz's tendency to overlook the impact of intrapsychic processes on institutional interactions.

In T. F. Main, one can see an important shift in focus. Main was concerned with the reciprocal nature of unconscious fears and primitive fantasy on the psychiatric ward and was more likely than Stanton and Schwartz to view patients as eliciting or contributing to the interpersonal and institutional environment. He was particularly interested in the evocation of omnipotence and aggression in staff members and in the staff's defensive use of treatment measures to disguise and discharge primitive emotions.

In a classic study (1957), Main described nurses who administered medication precisely at the moment when they could no longer tolerate the anxiety, impatience, guilt, hatred, and despair evoked by certain patients. When these same nurses learned to better accept their negative feelings, the need to rely on medication dropped dramatically. Interestingly, it increased again whenever new nurses joined the staff or when nurses were under heightened strain.

The primary focus in this study was a group of "special" patients who evoked extreme distress and regressive symptoms in their caretakers. Main discovered that certain nurses increasingly felt it their duty to attempt to gratify the demands these patients made for limitless caretaking. Each special patient seemed able to pick out a nurse who would be responsive to her needs and who could be trained to function as her narcissistic extension. For her part, the nurse came to feel a sense of aggrandizement, of being the only person sensitive enough and skilled enough to understand the therapeutic needs of her patient.

In every case, an increasing burden of guilt and ambivalence developed in the nurse as her efforts to provide omnipotent care failed. All of these patients grew steadily worse; attempting to create a world of delusional satisfactions only exacerbated their condition. As their patients deteriorated, the nurses began to show more outward signs of anxiety, depression, hatred, and resentment. In their omnipotence and their aggression, they had developed an "ailment" that mirrored the ailment of their patients.

It became apparent in retrospect that some of the special patients had actively evoked a split between their caretaker and the rest of the staff. Main was able to describe certain interpersonal measures employed by these patients to create factions in which a sense of specialness and exclusivity was fostered and in which communication with the opposing faction was discouraged.

This line of investigation is taken a step further by the work of Kernberg. Kernberg focuses on splitting and projective identification as processes by which the pathology of the primitive patient's internalized object relations becomes experienced in the countertransference and enacted in the hospital milieu.

In a 1987 clinical paper, Kernberg describes two patients who were able to make use of certain latent splits in the hospital organization to attack and defeat their therapist and to live out highly pathological internalized object relations. Interestingly, both of these individuals were considered "special." Like Main's patients, they had special needs and special connections that facilitated their destructive enactments. Also, like Main's patients, their success in evoking pathology in their caretakers and in their institution worked to their detriment.

In working with one of these patients, Kernberg experienced a transient paranoid reaction. His anxiety was so severe that he returned to the hospital after hours to discover if he was—as he feared—in danger of being dismissed from the staff because of his patient's behind-the-scenes manipulations. His belief that his "world as a unit chief was being destroyed . . . attacked and defeated" (p. 269) had been activated by the patient's deeply regressive behavior and by certain latent splits in the hospital's organization that rendered it vulnerable to splitting and projective identification.

The latent organizational splits were as follows: (1) between administrative psychiatrist and therapist, (2) between staff on the ward and hospital director (the latter subject to pressure from patients via influential family members), (3) between staff members holding different theoretical orientations or professional affiliations, (4) between the ward nurse and the director of nursing, (5) between black and white staff members. Each of these splits was directly or indirectly exacerbated by the patient, so that factions or individuals throughout the hospital experienced and/or acted out dissociated components of his internal world. In the language of the present study, these facilitating hospital arrangements can be thought of as countertransference structures.

COUNTERTRANSFERENCE STRUCTURE, COUNTERTRANSFERENCE DEFENSE

The material in this and subsequent chapters focuses on hospital organizational structures that ordinarily lie outside the scope of clinical investigation. Expanding on the insights of Stanton and Schwartz, Kernberg, and Main, I will attempt to show how both patients and staff make use of these structures to discharge and/or ward off transference/countertransference tensions. The reader may be surprised by the extent to which seemingly innocuous procedures and arrangements, having little apparent connection to clinical matters, are used in a reciprocal fashion to reduce anxiety and perpetuate primitive psychological processes.

Each countertransference experience is associated with a specific anxiety in the affected staff person, ranging in type and severity from neurotic to primitive. These anxieties foster the development of countertransference defenses, which may be understood as compromise formations that simultaneously express and ward off tensions. The relative weight of expressive and defensive elements varies. In the presentation of clinical material, I will indicate by the context which predominates in each case.

The term *countertransference defense* refers to an intrapsychic operation, the purpose of which is to establish or sustain the staff person's psychological equilibrium under conditions of threat. Hospital structures may facilitate this process. These structures augment defenses by providing a disguised institutionally sanctioned discharge channel and/or distancing procedure.

Although countertransference structures are sometimes recognized as problematic, efforts to reshape them are resisted in a manner reminiscent of resistances in the treatment hour. Their role in the transference/countertransference balance is seldom understood. This book is intended to alert clinicians to the manner in which these commonly accepted procedures and practices perpetuate regressive modes of experience.

PRIMITIVE PROCESSES IN THE MILIEU

In the present context, the term *primitive* refers to psychological states deriving from or primarily concerned with oral and narcissistic issues and to modes of functioning involving archaic ego states. In the sphere of internalized object relations, regression is marked by the predominance of poorly differentiated all-good and all-bad self and object representations that continually undergo elaboration and transformation through projective and introjective mechanisms. These part-objects carry poorly modulated libidinal and aggressive tensions (Kernberg 1976). They should be understood not simply as mental images but as having a dynamic functional dimension as described by Ogden (1986).

On the wards, deeply regressed patients evoke a psychological atmosphere defined by alienated polarities and the interpenetration of apparent opposites. It is important to understand this atmosphere in which endless boredom gives way inexplicably to unbearable tensions. Despite efforts to manage the flow, the staff is often carried into deep currents of primitive affect and disorienting manifestations of psychotic reality. The ward on some days presents itself as chaos incarnate and the staff finds itself buffeted by incomprehensible fears and misery. Then it subsides into deep apathy, which saps and immobilizes and robs the staff of its determination to help. These tides come and go, as the patients come and go, with new faces replacing the old and with few external markers to provide orientation.

The ambience of the ward lacks a dependable balance; it is at once volatile and frozen. Disparate elements combine or are transformed, disorienting the linear intelligence. In the world of shifting boundaries and magical transformations, identity— the first law of thought and the anchor of personal existence— yields to primary process, to fragmentation, to de-differentiation. Yet, the invocation of magic, the rawness, the flaring up of rage and fear inevitably subside into boredom and lethargy. A routinized and hopeless negation of existence reasserts itself in the blank stares, the obsessive nicotine hunger, the ritualistic and tireless begging, the pacing, the unceasing blare of the television.

Sometimes islands of relative clarity begin to coalesce out of the primary process matrix. The observer who can bear to see and feel will be appalled by the apparently bottomless hopelessness, a hopelessness that can engender paralysis and apathy in both staff and patients. Primitive patients experience themselves and their emotions as monstrous, alien, inhuman. Many look upon themselves as blood-sucking beasts, incapable of giving or receiving love. The ward is their isolation area,

their death camp, the material manifestation of their dehumanization.

Regressed patients devour their good internalized objects
or destroy them by turning them into persecutors. Driven by
poorly modulated hungers and fears, they hallucinate limitless
aggrandizement. Attempts to provide realistic assistance are
devalued and belittled. Staff members are drained, sucked dry,
experienced as malignant. They are buffeted by unsatisfiable
longings, frightened by murderous rage. Their motives are
constantly distorted and attacked so that they come at times to
doubt their capacity for goodness.

In working with primitive patients, one cannot fail to be
deeply shaken and dismayed by the realistic graveness of their
condition. Projective identifications heighten and distort the
experience of hopelessness. Hopelessness and its defensive
transformations constitute a sharing of the patient's inner
world of alienation, narcissistic rage, and unremitting hungers.

Our deeply disturbed patients evoke spoken and unspoken
fears. We fear at times for our physical safety and for our grip
on reality. We find ourselves experiencing shocking emotions
and fantasies. We come to loathe and fear certain patients as we
loathe and fear our own disavowed regressive impulses and
affects. Although we are frequently people who place great
stock in comprehension and mastery, our patients cause us to
grapple with confusion, disorientation, and panic. On the
ward, we soon gain a greater personal appreciation for the
bookish distinction between signal anxiety and anxiety that
threatens to overwhelm ego functions.

DEHUMANIZATION, SPLITTING, AND OMNIPOTENCE

An examination of characteristic defensive patterns provides some insight into the nature of the anxieties to which the
ward staff is exposed. Working with severely disturbed patients

regularly evokes derivatives of *dehumanization, splitting,* and *omnipotence.* These defenses, which mirror fundamental qualities of the patients' inner world, appear to have a special role in helping the staff maintain a more or less tenuous comfort zone. Sometimes in relatively pure culture but more often in combination, countertransference defenses utilizing these derivatives may be observed in individual staff members and in the workings of the milieu as a unit. Institutional structures that support, legitimize, or disguise enactments of dehumanization, splitting, and omnipotence tend to be highly valued and fiercely protected.

The case discussions focus on the manner in which severely disturbed patients elicit dehumanization, splitting, and omnipotence in their caretakers, and on the hospital structures that facilitate this process. Although other factors usually complicate the clinical picture, these will generally not be discussed in detail in order to limit the length of each presentation. Thus, the material may have a deceptively one-dimensional appearance, but I hope the reader will understand that the processes focused on are not the only operative ones.

The impulses and anxieties discharged and warded off by enactments of primitive ego states vary tremendously. In observing co-workers and their patients, only relatively limited aspects of the transference/countertransference constellation are discernible. However, much of my material is taken from supervised cases or cases examined in the course of a therapist's personal analysis; these can be elaborated in greater depth and detail.

TRANSFORMATIONS OF OMNIPOTENCE

It is usually understood that omnipotence plays a central role in the psychic life of regressed patients. What is less frequently noted is the extent to which the treatment of these patients may become infiltrated by more or less defended

enactments of omnipotence and its derivatives. Such enactments are very common. Often, one encounters wards where
they play a central role in the staff's efforts to maintain a
tolerable balance in the face of anxieties that cannot be contained and worked over in a more therapeutically productive
manner.

Primitive omnipotence has two main foci, or part-object
components: *Idealization* involves activation of all-good self
or object components and is associated with libidinal tensions,
especially oral incorporative fantasies and fantasies of limitless
gratification. *Persecutory omnipotence* involves activation of
all-bad self or object components and is associated with destructive rage and other aggressive tensions. Within each constellation, magical aggrandizement of poorly differentiated self
and object representations predominates. Each component
represents the obverse of the other and may, at any moment,
become transformed into the other.

The transformations of omnipotence can be seen with
unusual clarity in the transference psychosis of Mrs. O., a
schizophrenic woman in her late thirties. Mrs. O. had spent
much of her adult life caught up in the mental health
revolving door. Repeatedly, she had been committed to
state hospitals, medicated, and discharged to marginal
placements in the community, then rehospitalized after
another acute break. Eventually her husband divorced her.
She subsequently lost custody of her children and was
given up as hopelessly ill by her family. During her last
hospital admission, she worked with Dr. D. and asked to
continue in treatment with him after discharge.

Mrs. O. grew up with reclusive suspicious borderline
parents. Her passive frightened mother essentially ignored
her but adored her older brother, who could do no wrong
in the mother's eyes. When she noticed Mrs. O. at all, it
was to point out her inadequacies compared to the
brother. The mother was petrified with fear of her husband
but also helplessly dependent on him, apparently unable to

perform even the simplest household task without his supervision.

The father began to draw the patient into an incestuous relationship at an early age. This continued until she was eighteen. Mrs. O. was terrified of her father's rages and felt that she had to please him. She was certain that her mother would blame her or be unable to protect her if she confided in her. As soon as she was able, she left home to seek work in another city.

She quickly became involved in a loveless relationship with an abusive alcoholic, Mr. O. Their sexual activity disgusted and frightened her; it felt as though she was being savagely raped. They married after she became pregnant. In a few years, they had three children together. As their marriage deteriorated, Mrs. O. began to develop symptoms of depression. Then she experienced an episode of psychotic agitation, requiring involuntary hospitalization. With each subsequent episode, her condition worsened.

Mrs. O. had idolized her older brother, Ned. Although her clinging annoyed him, he sometimes permitted her to tag along after him on his adventures. Probably, he enjoyed and encouraged his sister's hero worship. Mrs. O. experienced him as fearless and rebellious, not intimidated by their father—everything she desperately wished to be.

Mrs. O. could not remember exactly when she began to fantasize a secret identity in which she became an adventurous boy herself. In the fantasy, she lived out all the real and imagined exploits of her fearless brother. Her body and mind were transformed. She was no longer trapped as Stella; she could become the strong and impetuous Steve. She was not delusional about her identity as "Steve," but she gave herself over to the fantasy with great fervor, preferring it at times to her actual existence.

Mrs. O. spent many sessions talking with Dr. D. about her contempt for women, especially for their weakness and passivity. At the same time, she was intensely frightened of homosexual longings in which she imagined being nurtured and provided for. Then, in the second year of therapy, she formed a powerful attachment to a clergyman who had taken an interest in her. It soon became apparent that she unconsciously experienced him as a powerful and intrusive father with whom she was living out a stormy incestuous liaison.

Mrs. O.'s overt functioning steadily improved for about four years. She increasingly took on important administrative responsibilities at her clergyman's church. She also discovered a special energy and talent for charitable work, which permitted her to provide care for the weak and hungry and to fight for justice for the downtrodden. She could hardly believe her newly found courage and competence.

The church and its members had become a beloved family, providing the patient with a level of support, protection, friendship, and understanding that was almost womb-like. Her unconsciously sexualized relationship with the clergyman seemed to balance the deeply regressive pull of the nurturing church community. Both deflected crucial elements of the transference away from Dr. D.

At this time, the patient began reporting dreams in which the church burned to the ground as a result of her negligence. She became increasingly anxious. Eventually, she made a small apartment for herself in the church so as to continually check that nothing was amiss. As her sense of impending disaster grew, she became unable to sleep. Her compulsive protective rituals were failing. Even a moment's lapse of vigilance might result in everything she loved being destroyed. She was certain she would be branded forever as criminally responsible.

Dr. D. attempted to help Mrs. O. understand that she feared harming or consuming those who cared for her. His interpretations were ineffectual. After a few months, the patient became acutely psychotic and suicidal and had to be readmitted to the ward. It was during this period of psychosis that details of her primitive omnipotence emerged more clearly.

Mrs. O. now believed that Dr. D. was God the Father and that she was his daughter. When the moment was ripe, he would provide her with a penis and she would be transformed into Jesus, his beloved Son. Everyone and everything on the ward was a manifestation of Dr. D.'s limitless goodness and power. The nurses, the attendants, and the patients were his angels, emanations of his divine glory watching over her and providing for her happiness. She wanted to perform fellatio on "his" attendants so as to imbibe his essence.

The idealized transference continued for several weeks. One afternoon, Mrs. O. was sitting in the ward recreation room, watching two patients play pool. One of them hit the ball with such force that it flew off the table, bounced on the tile floor, and then brushed slightly against the side of Mrs. O.'s foot. Since she was not hurt, nobody paid much attention to this incident.

The next morning, when Dr. D. walked on the ward, Mrs. O. attacked him without warning. She punched and flailed at him with her fists and nails, tried to bite him, kicked him in the groin. It was all he could do to hold her until help arrived. As she was led away to the seclusion room, she screamed that he was a demon, an evil spirit.

The seemingly trivial incident of the pool ball had triggered a massive shift in the patient's primitive internal object relations and a corresponding shift in the polarity of the omnipotent transference. Dr. D. had permitted harm to come to her. He must have tricked her. He was actually Satan, the personification of evil and destructiveness, her tormentor and persecutor.

Prior to her hospitalization, Mrs. O. had been living out the idealized transference in a manner congruent with her indulgent interpersonal reality. The church provided

maternal nurturing and protection, the feeling of acceptance into an all-encompassing Body of Christ, and an
opportunity to minister to persons who must have appeared more needy than herself.

Also provided was ongoing close contact with the
clergyman, whom the patient unconsciously experienced
as a powerful and seductive father whose love allowed her
to feel masculine, competent, independent, and fearless. It
also gave her the strength to moderate the deeply regressive pull of maternal longings. Her dreams of burning
down the church captured the rage and devouring need-
fulness that was split off from the experience of perfect
nurturing and protection. These feelings later became
manifested in the attack on Dr. D., who had—she felt—
seduced and cheated her.

SPLITTING AND OMNIPOTENCE ACTUALIZED
IN THE MILIEU

The transferences of Mrs. O. involved both relatively
compensated and floridly psychotic forms of idealization and
hostile/omnipotent control. One or both polarities of omnipotence—usually embedded in more or less realistic derivatives—
may make its way into the staff's treatment interventions and
interpersonal orientation, in accordance with the vicissitudes
of countertransference tensions. On many wards, the staff is
split into factions, one that identifies with the idealized and
another that identifies with the persecutory component of
a patient's omnipotence. Taking on components of the primitive patient's idealized part-object may protect the staff from
the patient's narcissistic rage. The opposing faction relies on
hostile/omnipotent control as a defense. Frequently, one sees
shifts from idealization to hostile control when the former fails
to contain the patient's rage.

The following case study illustrates an enactment of limitless nurturing in reaction to a schizophrenic patient's rage. At a critical juncture, nurturing shifted to omnipotent control. These enactments split the clinical staff and actualized the patient's internal split.

The patient, Mr. Y., was briefly hospitalized at a local psychiatric facility and was assigned to work with Dr. F. In their initial session, he made no secret of his feeling that the doctor existed primarily to satisfy his needs. It was clear from the moment he entered the office that their relationship would revolve around his limitless demands and around the intense interpersonal pressures he exerted to force Dr. F. into the mold of a narcissistic extension.

The manifest content of the session involved a request to make a number of calls from Dr. F.'s phone, as the patient had exhausted his money on previous calls from the ward's pay phone. The need to use the phone was experienced with great urgency, almost as a matter of life and death. It was clear that he expected immediate and complete satisfaction. It was also clear that he was capable of becoming quite explosive if his demands were not met. When he saw that his therapist wanted to talk with him about the use of the phone, rather than automatically comply, he became disgusted and left the interview.

Later in the day, during a seminar he was teaching, Dr. F. heard a loud imperative knock on the office door. Mr. Y. had returned to demand once again to use the phone. Dr. F. told him that he was busy, but that they could talk about the matter in about thirty minutes when the meeting would be over. The patient was unable to accept this postponement; he demanded that the meeting be ended immediately so that he could make his calls. The therapist reiterated that he would talk with him shortly. He then closed the door and resumed the seminar.

About five minutes later, everyone in the room was startled by a loud explosive sound, as though the door was being kicked down. With more than a little trepidation, Dr. F. again opened it to find the patient standing there, now obviously in a barely controlled rage, demanding to use the phone immediately. Dr. F. again told him when he would be available and closed the door. He then phoned the nursing station to arrange for the patient to be taken away from the office area until the meeting was over.

When he left the meeting, Dr. F. found Mr. Y. waiting for him a few steps down the corridor. He immediately began to attack the therapist verbally. He was now clearly experiencing Dr. F.'s failure to satisfy his needs as persecutory. His accusations were escalating in intensity and becoming more obviously delusional. Since it seemed apparent that his ability to maintain control was quite tenuous, the doctor did not invite Mr. Y. back to the office, but instead continued to talk with him in the corridor, where help was readily available if needed.

Dr. F. noticed almost immediately that the patient's anger seemed to be following a pattern. He would gradually become more angry and more paranoid as he raged. During this phase he would approach, as though on the verge of attacking. However, when he reached a certain emotional intensity and physical proximity, he would back off and de-escalate visibly. It occurred to Dr. F. that the patient was showing a partial capacity to protect him from his rage, to preserve him, to some limited extent, as a good object.

In talking with him in the corridor, the therapist was hoping to better understand the meaning of Mr. Y.'s preoccupation with the telephone. On a realistic level, the business he wanted to conduct seemed less than urgent, yet he was clearly experiencing it as a matter of life and death. Dr. F. also wanted to assess the extent to which it might be possible for the patient to see some value in talking to him despite the limitations inherent in the relationship. He felt fairly comfortable with the rhythm of their interaction, after having noted that the patient had entered with him into a process of creating a relatively protected therapeutic space.

To the casual observer, it must have appeared that Mr. Y. was on the verge of physically attacking his therapist. At the very least, his loud verbal outbursts were disrupting the atmosphere of the ward. In the midst of this apparently chaotic situation, the ward chief, whose office was a few steps down the corridor, opened his door and—with evident exasperation—intervened to restore order. He angrily told the patient that he was sick and tired of his yelling and complaining and that if he wanted to use the phone, he could make his calls from the nursing station. He then took him by the arm, escorted him to the ward, and sat him down in front of a phone, telling the nurses that he was to be permitted to make as many calls as were necessary to complete his business.

Later in the day, the ward chief expressed his sympathy to Dr. F. for having been the target of the patient's hostility and assumed that he was taking a day off later in the week because of the strain the patient had inflicted on him. He clearly felt he had rescued Dr. F. from an intolerable situation and had no idea he had disrupted a therapeutic interaction.

When he came to work the next morning, Dr. F. discovered that the chief had precipitously discharged the patient, to the evident relief of virtually the entire staff. It was apparent that the indulgent assistance he had provided was meant to temporarily placate Mr. Y. until it was possible to rid the ward of him once and for all.

In allowing him unlimited phone calls, the ward chief had enacted a role from the patient's primitive fantasy, that of idealized nurturer. In the magical/omnipotent world of primitive internalized object relations, the patient did not have to accept limited satisfactions or the consequences of his actions;

everything was to be provided for. When the ward chief later shifted to an aggressive form of omnipotent control, the patient's primitive internal world received further support and validation.

This case illustrates how primitive patients may evoke splits in the treatment team in which certain staff members are experienced as idealized and others as persecutory. These splits, if actualized via enactment, are then reintrojected in a manner that powerfully perpetuates part-object relatedness. The ward chief's willingness to provide unlimited phone calls rescued the patient from the frustrations inherent in reality. But, in so doing, he inadvertently confirmed the patient's worst fears about Dr. F.'s persecutory intentions and would have exposed the therapist to heightened danger had the patient remained on the ward.

GRATIFICATION AND LOSS

Mr. Y. experienced the milieu's inability to provide limitless gratification as an intentional attack. Paradoxically, it is from this juncture that treatment proceeds. The long-term goal is to help the primitive patient sustain access to a relatively benign experience of the therapist and the milieu during inevitable periods of frustration and loss. This level of functioning is achieved in very small increments and the extent to which it can be consolidated varies from patient to patient. Certain indications suggestive of consolidation can be seen in the case of Mr. L., the borderline patient discussed earlier in this chapter.

Mr. L. was typically unable to cope with serious disappointment without recourse to regressive defenses. During the years they worked together, his therapist—Dr. W.—witnessed him in the throes of many violent paranoid episodes precipitated by frustration and loss.

The patient was not altogether unaware of the feelings that fueled his propensity to react in this manner. Dr. W. once asked him about a quarrel he was having with a patient whom he had earlier been on relatively friendly terms with. He replied that the man was soon due to be discharged and that the only way he could deal with losing a friend was to fight with him; then the sadness would be replaced by anger.

Dr. W. saw a similar process occur whenever he was about to leave for vacation. Mr. L. would almost always find a way to pick a fight with him. The situation at times became quite dangerous because the patient's longings for Dr. W. were linked up with homosexual panic. He attempted to maintain balance by devaluing the therapist and accusing him of all sorts of misdeeds. There was always a danger he would escalate into a combative psychotic episode.

Mr. L. and Dr. W. terminated treatment under far from ideal circumstances, especially given the nature of the patient's problems. Dr. W. had been offered a prestigious academic appointment and had decided to resign his position on the hospital staff. As a result, he and Mr. L. had about six months in which to attempt to work through the ending of their treatment relationship.

Surprisingly, the patient did not become paranoid during this period. He continually reminded Dr. W. that he could easily do without him and that he had never been of much importance to him. But he was occasionally able to acknowledge that his therapist had at least attempted to help him, within the limits of his abilities. As the time for leaving grew closer, he began to make plans for his own discharge from the hospital. By rejecting the hospital, he was actively doing to the hospital what he unconsciously felt Dr. W. was doing to him.

About three years later, Dr. W. was walking in the corridors of another state hospital, introducing a group of residents to the ward staff. He felt a light tap on his shoulder and looked around to find Mr. L. smiling shyly at him. He said he had heard his therapist was on the ward and wanted to say hello. He had been hospitalized for several days and was now about to be discharged. Since Dr. W. last saw him, he had had several admissions, all of them relatively brief. He often thought about Dr. W., he said, and missed him at times.

Dr. W. was so surprised to see Mr. L. and to be approached in this friendly manner after their stormy and often frightening treatment relationship that he did not know quite how to respond. He was deeply touched but not prepared for the intensity of his feelings any more than he had been prepared for the patient's warm feelings. The best he could do was to tell Mr. L. that he had also thought about him and about their period of working together. They then turned—both feeling somewhat awkward—and went their separate ways.

According to the usual criteria, Mr. L. had probably not progressed very far. He continued to live an isolated existence on the fringes of society and periodically needed re-hospitalization. His increased capacity for whole object relatedness was not sufficient to keep him compensated at all times, but it may very well have been associated with other subtle changes in behavioral and psychological functioning. The relative brevity of his most recent hospitalizations was probably a reflection of these changes. Little of this would necessarily be apparent outside the context of a close working relationship.

For Mr. Y., on the other hand, it is almost certainly the case that his hospitalization made him sicker. His ability to tolerate object loss and the loss of magical omnipotence was extremely fragile. Tentative encounters with grief, dependency, or frustration triggered overwhelming fears of annihilation, necessitating regression to persecutory defenses.

Helping Mr. Y. achieve a more integrated and secure level

of functioning required a treatment in which limits were regulated and acknowledged and their meanings explored. By validating the patient's denial of loss and human limitation, his experience in the hospital supported omnipotent defenses and exacerbated the generalized ego dysfunction that results from reliance on splitting.

Setting realistic limits plays a key role in helping manage primitive aggression. In working with patients who experience narcissistic rage—such as Mr. L. or Mr. Y.—it is crucial that the therapist takes measures to prevent behavior from escalating out of control. Secure controls protect the patient from becoming overwhelmed. Just as importantly, they help establish a degree of physical security that allows the therapist's empathy and observing ego to function. In essence, what is required is a level of safety that permits verbal expression of primitive ego states but limits destructive behavior.

As the work proceeds, the therapist will be repeatedly exposed to verbal or behavioral derivatives of primitive drives, especially to demands for limitless nurturing and to the frightening rage that can flare up when it is not provided. This encounter of human limitation and primitive imperative is a key matrix out of which characteristic countertransference anxieties and defenses develop.

The therapist may be sorely tempted to relieve his anxiety by placating the patient, thus buying off the negative transference, or he may wish to retaliate or emotionally disengage himself. By containing and internally working over these and other feelings and action-tendencies evoked in the course of the therapeutic encounter, the therapist offers the patient a more mature and adaptive manner of coping with drive-laden tensions. These more mature coping functions become available for reintrojection, thus interrupting the cycle of projection and reintrojection of primitive processes.

If the therapy progresses, the patient becomes increasingly able to hold the therapist in his mind as a good object during periods of loss. Interpretations, especially integrative interpretations, become increasingly important at this stage. Slowly, the patient may come to recognize the inevitability of limited satisfactions, to grieve realistic losses and limitations, and to reduce dependency upon magical/omnipotent defenses and transformations.

Working at close quarters with primitive transferences in the manner I have described is extremely difficult. Determined efforts to contain disturbing tensions notwithstanding, treatment interventions frequently become more or less infiltrated by hostile/omnipotent or idealized part-object components. Limit setting and other managerial procedures are especially predisposed in this direction. Providing appropriate management is technically and emotionally a daunting challenge. Throughout this book, I will be discussing treatments that failed or were badly compromised due to a blurring of boundaries between management and enactment. Such errors are not always easy to recognize, even in retrospect. When one is caught up in the emotions that evoke them, such enactments take on a compelling driven quality, so that their appropriateness may seem self-evident.

DEVELOPMENTAL HISTORY OF A
COUNTERTRANSFERENCE STRUCTURE

The following case study illustrates how a therapist's anxiety-laden identification with her patient's primitive part-object contributed to the development of a more or less permanent hospital structure, one that supported defensive distancing and provided an illusion of omnipotent control.

The outpatient department at a large private hospital erected a complicated and expensive system of steel doors and impenetrable Plexiglas barriers in order to control access to the secretarial and clinical staff areas. In order to complete this security system, concrete walls had to be torn down and the waiting room relocated. A video monitoring system and remote control lock were installed so that the outpatient secretary could admit or bar patients from the office area without coming into contact with them.

The security system was installed after an episode in which a frightening violent paranoid patient, who had been intermittently coming to the outpatient department for many years, appeared in the hospital one day carrying what he claimed was a box of explosives and threatening to blow up himself, his therapist, and everyone else present. The patient was able to make his way to the outpatient area, causing panic and confusion among the persons he encountered on the way. He then barricaded himself in an office, smashed out a window with a chair, and threatened to jump. He also threatened to set off the explosive device if anyone tried to enter the room.

The police were called and arrived almost immediately. The patient was thought to be extremely dangerous and probably came very close to being shot. Fortunately, the police were able to persuade him to surrender without using force. It eventually turned out that the box he was carrying contained a relatively harmless device capable of producing only a loud noise. In retrospect, the danger posed by this incident was clearly more suicidal than homicidal, although no one could have known this until after events ran their course.

The paranoid patient's therapist, Ms. B., had been badly abused and intimidated by him for many years. The patient had grown dependent on her and always returned during periods of crisis or decompensation. Ms. B. felt herself in an impossible dilemma. The more she attempted to placate the patient by acceding to his demands, the more the demands escalated. The situation was clearly out of control. The patient treated her as his personal slave. She felt unable to set realistic limits without running the risk of precipitating a dangerous attack. She wished she could somehow get rid of her impossible burden, but the patient's obviously desperate need for her made her feel guilty and frightened if she attempted to change the nature of the relationship.

After the incident of the bogus bomb, the patient was committed to an inpatient unit for several weeks. When he recompensated, Ms. B. referred him to a therapist at a community mental health clinic in a nearby town.

In the course of his treatment there, a familiar constellation of psychological processes became apparent. The patient's intimidating behavior was tied to an identification with a physically and psychologically abusive father who had terrorized the entire family throughout the patient's childhood and adolescence. By causing others to experience his disavowed and split-off passivity, impotence, and terror, the patient was more able to feel identified with the powerful aggressive father.

Ms. B. had for years been the recipient of the patient's projective identifications. To placate him, she attempted to satisfy endless demands for unscheduled appointments, soothing medications, and active "supportive" interventions needed to rescue the patient from a variety of perceived emergencies. Thus, an idealized transference was enacted that held his attacks at bay. Throughout this course of treatment, Ms. B. was silently living out the patient's split-off self-experience of terror, devaluation, and helplessness.

Ms. B. was instrumental in obtaining the impenetrable security system for the outpatient department. The impact of the failed treatment had made an indelible impression on her and many others in the hospital. The security system offered a reassuringly dependable auxiliary ego-defense, establishing an external barrier that seemed to bolster badly strained internal sources of safety and security.

Once in place, the steel and Plexiglas system functioned as an ever-present reminder that patients could be dealt with at a physical and emotional distance, according to the dictates of superior power. Staff members in the throes of perplexing or anxiety-laden clinical interactions could readily see in it the hospital's and their colleagues' silent affirmation of treatment methods utilizing derivatives of omnipotent control.

A massive emphasis on power-oriented security arrangements often signals poorly contained anxiety and a failure to implement sound clinical practices. In the present example, the security system was built in reaction to a real and potentially disastrous assault on the hospital and its staff, but it cannot be adequately understood without reference to the mishandled treatment relationship.

The paranoid patient's alarming acting out culminated years of emotional turmoil and acting out by his therapist. Along the way, each crisis precipitated by his limitless demands and narcissistic rage was temporarily and tenuously resolved by an enactment in which the therapist mollified the patient and abnegated her own personhood, identifying with the patient's degraded, helpless, and enslaved part-object. The crisis resulting from this course of treatment can be understood as a final escalation, the patient's ultimate attempt to obtain omnipotent control and satisfaction. It was followed by a corresponding defensive shift to omnipotent control by the therapist, a shift that frequently occurs when idealized enactments fail to contain primitive tensions. The projections and part-object identifications that fueled the crisis were never examined.

SUPEREGO MEDIATED OMNIPOTENT CONTROL

Omnipotent control in the countertransference often involves a heightening of superego aggressivity. Frequently, it is intensified and primitivized by identifications with projected superego precursors that the disturbed patient is unable to contain internally. Superego mediated derivatives of omnipotent control may become highly valued in interactions with patients who overstimulate sexual or aggressive urges. By controlling the patient, staff members attempt to regain more secure control of their own impulses. Patients may be experienced not as differentiated and complex human beings, but as external representations of intolerable needs and fantasies.

A withdrawn and preoccupied young woman with a history of numerous hospitalizations typically began to emerge from autism by forming tentative attachments to various male patients. These attachments consisted of sitting silently together in the TV area, holding hands while walking the corridor, and exchanging an occasional kiss or embrace.

These activities were harmless and would hardly have been noticed outside the ward. More importantly, this young woman's "romantic" attachments were not primarily sexual, but represented an anxiety-laden effort to emerge from a state of utter isolation, self-loathing, and hopelessness, and to reestablish contact with a world of responsive objects.

Many staff members, however, reacted to her reintegrative efforts with great hostility, condemnation, and overreactive control measures. Her attractiveness and seductive manner elicited intensely powerful responses. Unconsciously excited male staff members were anxious and threatened. Certain female staff members resented and envied the patient's hold on the men and employed control measures in the service of retribution.

The staff tended to regard sexual feelings toward patients as alien and unacceptable; thus, they had great difficulty in becoming aware of such feelings. They also had difficulty differentiating their own sexual needs and anxieties from the patient's very different experience of sexuality. In response to their discomfort, they attempted to regulate every sexually disturbing aspect of the patient's appearance and behavior.

As distinct from appropriate and realistic management, omnipotent control is regarded here as involving the belief that all aspects of persons, impulses, fantasy, and feeling are susceptible to intrapsychic or behavioral control. It frequently involves a blurring or loss of boundaries between self and other, internal and external. The paranoid individual's dread that alien hallucinatory presences have taken over his mind and behavior illustrates a very primitive form of hostile omnipotent control. Another example is provided by Kohut (1971), who describes narcissistic self-objects who are experienced as susceptible to control in the same manner and degree that one exercises control over one's own limbs.

In the case of the seductive young woman, the blurring of boundaries was evident in the staff's failure to differentiate between its own and the patient's sexuality. Underlying magical omnipotence could also be seen in the exaggerated quality of the management measures taken. These were directed not at limited and specific areas of conduct that might present a clear and present danger, but seemed intended to rid the milieu of all derivatives of sexual tension. The fact that they were administered with an air of angry and offended vindictiveness was further indication of their countertransference origins.

DEHUMANIZATION

The ward staff described above was unable to recognize the feelings and fantasies stirred up by the seductive young woman in part because it was felt that psychiatric patients were beyond the pale of sexual interest. The countertransference defense of dehumanization may have contributed to this feeling.

I am reminded of this possibility by a conversation I recently had with a therapist at a local private psychiatric facility. The therapist was complaining about a nurse on her staff who was rumored to be dating a former patient. She objected to this alleged relationship on the grounds that psychiatric patients should be viewed as a "different species" as far as sexual feelings were concerned. This notion probably helped to ward off anxiety triggered by inevitable and commonly occurring sexual attractions.

The dehumanization of hospitalized psychiatric patients was described in vivid detail by Goffman from a social-psychological perspective (1961). In contrast, the emphasis here is on dehumanization as a primitive mental state involving certain characteristic regressive distortions of the self-representation, and as an interpersonal orientation through which a hospital staff may attempt to create psychological distance from primitive patients.

The concept of dehumanization is meant to convey the painful sense of hopeless alienation from the world of human connectedness experienced by deeply regressed individuals. In a concrete and literal manner that often shocks the therapist who comes to know them in depth, these individuals experience themselves as nightmarish beasts or monsters. Their alienation is based on a sense of irremediable badness deriving from an unconscious or partially conscious awareness of rage, envy, and a capacity to devour and destroy internal objects.

Several years ago, while sitting in the nursing station of a local state facility where I occasionally conducted psychological assessments, I noticed some consternation among a group of nurses and attendants at the other end of the room. Apparently, a patient had come to the nursing station a moment earlier, picked up a comb that had been lying on a table, and was standing by the doorway combing his hair with it.

The nurse whose comb had been taken was berating the patient, telling him that patients were never to touch anything that belonged to her. It was clear that whatever professionalism she might ordinarily have at her disposal had been washed away in a flood of emotion. The other staff members seemed to share her view that something disgusting and outrageous had occurred; they also seemed amused by her predicament.

The patient was a disheveled and unkempt man whom I had known several years earlier when he was hospitalized at a facility where I was on staff. He had been mentally ill for many years, had received repeated psychiatric hospitalizations, and lived the life of a street derelict during the intervals between admissions. If ever a person existed who, by his appearance and strangeness of manner, conveyed the impression of living outside the radius of normal human existence, it would be this man. However, I knew him to be, in his own odd way, highly attuned to his surroundings. In the interaction I had just witnessed, he had elicited cruelty and devaluation by drawing the nurses into enacting a split-off component of his internal drama.

The patient had taken the comb to make himself more acceptable, more like the clean and well-groomed nurses who seemed to be in charge of his life. He had been, a moment before, happily combing his hair by the nursing station door. As the group scolded and laughed about the purloined comb, one could see his mood gradually deflating. He tried to return it, but the nurse refused to take it back, as though she could not bear to touch it. His merely having physical contact with the comb had defiled it. The nurses, of course, did not consciously wish to convey that the patient was repugnant to them, but the intensity of their feelings was unmistakable.

The cruelty inflicted on this man reflected the perception that he was a creature so alien as to no longer be part of the human community, incapable of experiencing recognizable human emotions. This judgment mirrored the patient's split-off self-loathing and can be understood as an identification with it.

To some extent, he had precipitated the rejection. He knew this group of nurses well and was unlikely not to have understood on some level their probable reaction to his behavior.

Dehumanizing the patient also alleviated anxieties originating from a number of intrapsychic levels within the staff. As I listened to the nurses' conversation, I noted that the patient was associated with issues having primarily to do with feelings of narcissistic vulnerability and with anality.

For certain of these staff members, the patient's repugnant appearance and strange mannerisms activated anxieties having to do with self-esteem, racial vulnerability, and social acceptance. The nurses were black, as was the patient. His attempt to identify with them was rejected because it evoked a commonality that was intolerable. By rejecting his need for acceptance and by distancing themselves from the pain he experienced as an outsider, they rejected similar feelings in themselves.

The nurses also appeared to identify the patient with filth and anality. Once he used the comb, it became repugnant and untouchable; it now carried his dirt, which might rub off on the staff. Certain of the nurses unconsciously equated being dirtied with the fear of losing control or becoming crazy.

The unconscious experience of mental patients as excrement is much more common than one might imagine. I recently attended a ward conference during which the clinical staff—consisting of several psychologists, social workers, and a psychiatrist—was discussing a number of elderly patients who were experiencing urinary incontinence. In the course of this discussion, it became clear that the staff's devaluing references to the foul odor on the ward referred as much to the patients themselves as to the actual odor.

One staff member, for example, joked that the ward was beginning to smell like a kennel. The others laughed at this comparison and someone noted that the hospital would soon have to apply to the American Kennel Association for accreditation. These comments, which almost everyone at the conference seemed to find amusing, warded off powerful anxieties having to do with becoming old, debilitated, dirty, and crazy.

As is the case with splitting and omnipotence, dehumanization is basically a primitive defense. Its presence is frequently a signal that relatively regressed transference/countertransference tensions have become activated. Regressive tensions may constitute the primary emotional significance of an activated countertransference or may coexist with a neurotic level of anxiety. For example, in each of the vignettes just given, fear of becoming overwhelmed or psychotic or helpless coexisted with anxiety around developmentally more advanced anal issues.

I will now describe a dehumanizing hospital procedure that kept disturbed patients at a physical and psychological distance, moving them about as though they were lifeless, disconnected objects. This attenuation of interpersonal relatedness was rigidly defended because it helped highly threatened hospital staff members distance themselves from the emotions evoked by close working contact with these patients.

It may be helpful to begin by providing a context in which the clinical material can be better examined: For most of the severely disturbed patients who were affected by the procedure in question, discontinuity of relatedness was a pervasive feature of social and interpersonal existence as well as of intrapsychic organization. Many were alienated from their families, had lost their homes and jobs, and were dependent on disability benefits. Those who sustained family or community ties often seemed to be attached by the most tenuous of threads, living within extremely chaotic, deprived, or undependable social contexts.

A large proportion of these patients were caught up in a cycle of repeated psychiatric hospitalizations. Between admissions, many were placed in group care homes in the community. Conditions were often abysmal. The practice of warehousing psychiatric patients in minimally funded private homes, often in impoverished crime-infested neighborhoods, cared for by persons with minimal training, and provided with painfully inadequate support services conveys the full weight of the community's fear and devaluation of these patients.

The mental health revolving door typically involved repeated hospitalizations and repeated placements. Following each placement, patients were likely to find themselves assigned to a new outpatient clinic. Thus, the opportunity to form stable and enduring treatment relationships was also lacking. The milieu I am describing is one in which the continuity of family, community, work, and treatment ties was severely disrupted and in which the satisfaction of minimal subsistence needs was far from dependable.

This pervasive fragmentation was seriously exacerbated by the admissions procedure at a local state hospital where many of these patients were periodically treated:

> When a newly admitted patient arrived at the hospital in question, a rotation list was consulted to determine which therapist was next in line for an assignment. Unless patients had been discharged within the past month, they were automatically assigned to the next therapist on the list.

> It seemed to some on the staff that this procedure violated a basic requirement of continuity of care. A large number of the hospital's patients received repeated hospitalizations but relatively few were readmitted within one month. Thus, most were assigned to a new therapist upon each admission. In response to the problem, several therapists proposed that all patients should be routinely assigned to their previous therapist, except in special circumstances.

> The proposal was circulated among all the inpatient therapists and administrators and was discussed on the

wards with members of the various treatment teams. Administrators, at least initially, were fairly receptive to the idea. Many therapists and other members of the ward staff, however, were aghast. All sorts of objections were raised and discussed in staff meetings, but it quickly became clear that providing realistic information had no impact on the fears that were being voiced.

Under normal conditions, mental health professionals could be expected to welcome an opportunity to enhance continuity of care and build long-term treatment relationships. It was evident, however, that staff members were clinging fiercely to the old admissions policy. Everyone seemed convinced that their ward was going to be singled out as a dumping ground for the most disturbed and unmanageable patients. The degree of panic and paranoia was remarkable. The possibility of no longer being able to rely on the anonymity and disengagement afforded by the revolving door process was clearly having a disorganizing effect on the ego functions of many staff members.

As discussions dragged on, one could notice a shift in the attitude of administrators who had previously been supportive or at least relatively noncommittal. After a somewhat heated staff meeting, two administrators privately took aside one of the initiators of the proposal to ask why he persisted with an idea that was obviously so disturbing. Couldn't he see what he was doing to his co-workers? The administrators seemed to understand on some level that the old policy provided a distancing function, without which the staff experienced panic, projection, and other signs of regression.

It eventually became apparent that the hospital was going to deal with its dilemma by burying the admissions proposal in committee for further study. About two years later, when it seemed certain that no action was going to be taken, the matter was brought to the attention of the hospital director. His response was to extend the period of continuity from one to six months. Thus, a large number of returning patients continued to be assigned by rotation. The underlying fears and fantasies that fueled rejection of the original proposal were never openly discussed or acknowledged.

In Chapter 1, the concepts of countertransference defense and countertransference structure were introduced. This was followed by an examination of clinical material illustrating how derivatives of dehumanization, splitting, and omnipotence infiltrate hospital procedures. I have also attempted, in a limited way, to re-create here the atmosphere of regression and primitive anxiety within the treatment milieu, so as to convey some sense of the psychological tenuousness and threat that engenders and supports defensive structures.

Countertransference-infiltrated procedures represent a residue of wasted potential. Their existence testifies to the staff's capacity for deeply felt identification with primitive patients, with their hopeless alienation, magical omnipotence, and sense of imminent danger. But this empathic recognition too often fails to engender a sense of kinship and collaboration; instead it can set in motion a process of radical disengagement from the patient and from the therapeutic task.

2

Psychiatry and the Medical Model

The literature in psychology and psychiatry includes numerous discussions of the medical model of mental illness and treatment. Theoretical, philosophical, historical, and clinical perspectives are represented. In tone, this body of writing ranges from dispassionate and scholarly to frankly polemical. In this chapter, the topic is approached from a practice-oriented point of view and with a definite agenda in mind. In the material to follow, I attempt to demonstrate that certain widely held interpretations of the medical model function in the treatment milieu to provide conceptual and emotional support for a range of countertransference-based defenses and enactments.

As defined here, the model consists of several interrelated elements. Of these, perhaps the most central is its often single-minded focus on disease or disease processes. Because this approach has contributed to immense scientific and therapeutic progress in physical medicine, it is perhaps only natural to assume it can be as useful in the realm of psychological disorders and that it can be applied without major alterations or reservations. However, there is strong reason to believe that the medical model feeds into powerful tendencies to retreat from connectedness with psychiatric patients as whole living persons. Relating primarily to a disease entity all too easily comes to support the dehumanization of those who "have" the disease.

The medical model does not regard disease solely as a phenomenon to be studied with cool scientific detachment. One of its chief foundations is an emotionally potent commitment to the belief that disease is an evil, an adversary to be challenged and conquered, an enemy of human well-being. Its guiding image is of the physician—in the likeness of a soldier—warring upon a crafty and malignant opponent.

However, an adversarial stance is difficult to reconcile with what we know to be the functional dimension of mental and emotional illness. Psychiatric symptoms seem entirely pathological only if we adopt an exclusively external observational perspective. From the standpoint of the patient however, symptoms are valued because they sustain and comfort and offer protection from further regression.

A too aggressive stance toward mental illness readily degenerates into an adversarial stance toward persons who are ill. Throughout this book I report and examine instances of unconscious attacks carried out by hospital staff members who thought they were aggressively treating symptoms of disease. To the extent that the medical model serves as a conceptual justification for such enactments, it can be regarded as a countertransference-enhancing structure.

A third crucial component is the dominant—even exalted—role reserved for the physician. This notion involves a dyadic relationship between a scientist/healer wielding a therapeutic armamentarium and a disease entity that is to be controlled or conquered. The allocation of essentially exclusive authority and prestige to the physician adds to certain characteristic difficulties in the relationship between doctor and mental patient and between doctor and other members of the treatment team. The material to follow examines how physician pre-eminence and the institutional structures derived from it contribute to splitting and enactments of omnipotence and devaluation.

The medical model tends to be protected and esteemed by members of all the mental health professions, physicians and nonphysicians alike. Its influence is usually so persuasive and so intertwined with innumerable ordinary actions and modes of thought as to be hardly noticed, much less seriously questioned. One important reason for this remarkable ascendancy is the model's efficacy in facilitating the discharge and warding off of primitive tensions.

The focus here is on the misuse of the model, the readiness with which it is exaggerated and distorted in the service of countertransference enactment and defense. However, if it is as amenable to distortions and if these are as potent a source of injury and failure as the material in these pages would seem to suggest, then the ideas put forth here may bear on the larger question of the suitability of the model in its traditional form for the treatment of persons with mental and emotional disorders.

PSYCHIATRIC DOMINANCE

It is difficult for a psychologist to speak to the issue of dysfunctional psychiatric authority in a manner that is not suspect. Working in an ancillary capacity in many psychiatric hospitals, psychologists clearly have a personal and professional interest in enhancing their standing vis-à-vis psychiatry.

The task of achieving some degree of objectivity is made even more difficult by the fact that personal relations among members of the various mental health professions may be distorted by complex irrational tensions emanating from patients. As a result, sorting out the origins of feelings such as envy, resentment, and competitiveness is daunting, to say the least.

However, readers of psychoanalytic case discussions are not altogether unaccustomed to such complications, especially in the realm of countertransference phenomena. It seems unavoidable that an author's emotional involvement in a topic puts an extra burden on readers, who must continually assess the author's feelings and perceptions and compare them to their own clinical experience. I am especially hopeful that psychiatrists will make this effort as they read this material. Although the ideas advanced in this section may coincide at times with the self-interest of nonmedical practitioners, their potential significance lies in the fact that they address an oridinarily unnoticed dimension of interdisciplinary relationships in the psychiatric hospital, one that can easily be misunderstood if one focuses too exclusively on the manifest content of turf battles and power struggles.

The following case material is taken from a variety of hospitals, including both state and private facilities. Although many differences could be noted among the wards described here, all had hierarchical organizational structures. Psychiatrists were at the head of the team and the ward, exercising overall authority and responsibility. Other team members served in a more or less ancillary capacity.

In practice, the lines of authority and responsibility were usually more ambiguous and complex than indicated by formal organizational arrangements. But exceptions and complications notwithstanding, the position of ward psychiatrist invariably carried a singular administrative, clinical, and emotional weight. Any attempt to understand the psychological tensions and balances operating in these settings must begin with an examination of the pivotal role played by psychiatrists.

To begin, it should be obvious that the term *psychiatric dominance* is misleading unless certain qualifications are added. Perhaps most importantly, the pre-eminent position of psychiatrists cannot be understood simply as a mandate imposed from above on unwilling subordinates. Although it in part reflects the traditional manner in which medical settings are organized, psychiatric dominance is most accurately viewed as a highly complex phenomenon, with intrapsychic and interpersonal—as well as organizational—dimensions.

Most staff members at the facilities surveyed here more or less ambivalently supported the leading role assigned to psychiatrists in the ward hierarchy. Shifts in the polarity of the ambivalence were quite striking and easy to observe. For example, staff members tended to put immense pressure on "their" psychiatrist to live up to exaggerated or magical expectations, especially during moments of great tension and anxiety. At other times, conscious and unconscious envy, rivalry, and resentment might be the operative emotions.

A few psychiatrists actively sought heightened authority and prestige; most accepted the mantle with misgivings. In either case, idealization of the psychiatrist constituted an important component of defensive operations in the milieu, often becoming linked up with unconscious fears, fantasies, and enactments of omnipotence, splitting, and devaluation by patients and staff members.

The following clinical material is drawn from a ward where aggrandizement of the psychiatrist played a crucial role in maintaining a countertherapeutic equilibrium, warding off anxieties in staff, patients, and probably in the psychiatrist herself. The great esteem in which this practitioner was held reflected more than an appreciation of her many admirable qualities. On an unconscious level, it functioned to sustain a split in which defensive idealization and devaluation were repeatedly lived out in the milieu.

The ward in question was one of several adult units in a large state psychiatric hospital that I refer to here as Greenwood Retreat. The interpersonal orientation on this ward was often marked by a subtle but unnecessary harsh ness and authoritarianism. These attitudes were difficult to understand in the context of the relatively favorable manifest conditions of work. In contrast to many of the state hospital settings described here, the ward was well staffed and efficient, the patients were not typically overwhelmingly sick or dangerous, and caseloads were of a manageable size. Nevertheless, a preponderance of the staff seemed to have reached an unconscious consensus manifested by widespread reliance on devaluing attitudes and practices.

A quiet but powerful effort was exerted to sustain the consensus and draw new staff members into it. This could be seen clearly in ward meetings, where one could not fail to be aware of subtle pressures to participate in the jokes and belittling remarks made at the expense of patients. Probably, few of the participants recognized the demeaning tone of these meetings; many would have felt hurt or offended or misunderstood had it been pointed out to them.

The meetings were called the "mark down," a term that was meant to refer to the process of discussing a list of patients and recording medical orders for each in the chart, but that inadvertently revealed much about the meeting's unconscious agenda. The ward psychiatrist, Dr. K., presided. Subtle variations in her tone as she read each patient's name elicited an empathic response from the assembled staff. If her manner was derisive or long-suffering, for example, the name would trigger a chorus of snickers or slightly belittling humorous remarks. Her description of the misfortunes and foibles of certain patients might produce a similar reaction. The group dynamics in these meetings were such that newcomers found it difficult to resist being drawn into the ambience of hurtful distancing humor.

In most respects, however, Dr. K.'s orientation was kindly, self-effacing, and nurturing. She gave her patients soothing medication and a good deal of maternal affection when they were in distress and scolded them in a good-natured fashion when they failed to show improvement. The patients tended to idolize her. During periods when she conducted clinical interviews, they lined the hall outside her office, milling about or sitting on the floor, waiting for the good luck to be granted an audience.

At times, however, Dr. K.'s equanimity and good humor failed her. Then a surprising capacity to lash out in an irritated fashion against patients who had frustrated or disappointed her became more apparent.

In one such incident, she was unable to contain her exasperation with a chronic drug abuser, a man who was periodically admitted to the ward but who typically returned to a self-destructive way of life within a few days or weeks of being discharged. On this admission, the patient presented as depressed, hopeless, and suicidal. Dr. K. had worked long and hard with the patient and was very upset with his repeated backsliding, especially with his refusal to leave his wife, whom she blamed for luring him back to drugs.

After a few days on the ward, Dr. K. took the patient into her office and told him, in her usual humorous scolding style, that he had "two chances left in life, slim or none," depending upon whether or not he would leave his wife. Probably, her intention was to shock the patient into constructive action, but the gloomy prognostication had an opposite effect. The patient felt the harshness of the remark but was unable to hear the concern for his welfare that was also deeply felt.

When he left the hospital a few days later, the patient felt more confused and desperate than ever. He continued the pattern of separation and reconciliation with his wife and continued to abuse drugs. About a year later, it became known that he was attempting to obtain controlled substances by forging prescriptions under the name of Dr. K.

Dr. K. experienced her patients as making never-ending demands on her. Most typically, she attempted to gratify them. In fact, she had the reputation of being unable to say no to anyone. By providing nurturing, Dr. K. may have been making reparations for ego-dystonic aggression. But by overextending herself, she probably increased her susceptibility to inevitable frustration, disappointment, and irritation.

The doctor's usual courtly courtesy, her kindness, and the high esteem in which she was held coexisted with a certain aloof and inaccessible personal remoteness that gently but firmly held others in a position of subordination, creating a line that could not be readily crossed.

One could observe the distinctness of this boundary during staff meetings. Dr. K. sat behind a large and imposing desk, holding court for the assembled staff members, some of whom literally sat at her feet, mirroring the position of the patients who so devotedly sat waiting for her in the hallway. She held forth with wit and good humor, sometimes at the expense of patients but never with the least lack of kindness for those present. Periodically, she would benevolently give away tickets to concerts or other cultural events. The air of noblesse oblige was unmistakable.

What was most striking about this psychiatric unit was the contrast between the usually benign personality of Dr. K. and the devaluing atmosphere that could so frequently be observed on the ward. The head nurse, Mr. G., who had worked with Dr. K. for many years, was a very determined and power-oriented individual who readily became confrontational, demeaning, and sarcastic when he felt challenged or threatened. He believed in maintaining strict control and encouraged his staff to identify with his authoritarian and infantilizing interpersonal style.

The nursing staff's approach was not always aggressive by any means, but the potential for overly punitive measures was almost always present or at least implied. This stance was organized around a highly cathected system of rules and punishments. One could not help but notice that rules were enforced with an unmistakable sense of satisfaction, at times of triumph. Attempts to work clinically with noncompliant patients were resented, as though the clinician was depriving certain staff members of a highly valued function. The view of patients as disobedient children was concretized by a large chalk board in the middle of the ward on which were recorded the names and infractions of all who were currently under punishment.

The incongruity between the punitive devaluing ward and the benign idealized psychiatrist was more apparent than real. In actuality, the two factions depended on one another to sustain a crucial unconscious equilibrium.

The ward staff tended to act out openly punitive behavior that Dr. K. was unlikely to indulge in herself but that seemed to have her implicit approval. In a sense, her ego-dystonic aggression was displaced to the ward, where it constituted the predominant regime, permitting Dr. K. to maintain a nurturing idealized stance above the fray, dispensing soothing elixirs and wise advice. Mr. G.'s relatively open hostility and the structures of punishment and regimentation he had constructed helped keep Dr. K. the center of love and admiration by deflecting negative transferences toward the nursing staff.

Many members of the ward staff were emotionally dependent on this split. Punishing and controlling patients served as a psychological regulatory mechanism that helped staff externalize and then attack dystonic needs and emotions. Any organizational arrangement that facilitated this process was highly valued and resistant to change.

The need to aggrandize Dr. K. was also part of the system of countertransference regulation. The degree of consolation and soothing experienced by staff members who basked in her reflected omnipotence was quite impressive. The fantasy that she possessed a magic elixir was strong and close to consciousness. Conceptions of treatment—no matter how cautiously introduced—that called her magical powers into question were more often than not rejected out of hand because they threatened to bring feelings of helpless, futility, and other dystonic emotions closer to consciousness.

In some respects, this ward might be regarded as a model of efficiency. Certainly, its outward aspect compared favorably with the openly chaotic conditions that prevailed at other settings described here. What was most interesting however, was the enduring and complex psychological equilibrium that had evolved. With its inherent structural split, the ward constituted a fertile medium into which primitive patients could project, live out, and then reintroject split-off idealized and attacking part-objects.

In the present context, it is important to emphasize that Dr. K., as well as most members of the staff, regarded her idealized position as an appropriate, necessary, and altogether unremarkable expression of physician pre-eminence. It was a matter so taken for granted as to be virtually absent from ordinary conscious perception and clinical discourse. To the extent that the medical model supported this notion, it played a role in disguising and perpetuating enactments of primitive part-object relatedness on this ward.

OMNIPOTENCE AND DISTANCING IN A PSYCHIATRIC TRAINING PROGRAM

The enactment of omnipotence—in one or another of its transformations—can be viewed as an attempted solution to a multiplicity of intrapsychic, interpersonal, and organizational problems in the milieu. In the material above, idealization of Dr. K. played a role in augmenting the ward staff's regulation of anxiety and self-esteem, helped to distance Dr. K. from ego-dystonic aggression, and facilitated patients' efforts to split the staff into opposing factions. A convergence of defensive and expressive needs resulted in the development of an inter-locking configuration of actions and modes of experience that constituted a stable and highly effective countertransference structure.

In contrast, the structure to be examined next did not gradually evolve in response to unconscious transference/countertransference tensions. Instead, it continued to serve many of the educational purposes for which it had been designed. However, at times it also took on a parallel function far removed from its realistic purposes. The following material will illustrate how certain characteristics of a residency training program inadvertently supported reliance on distancing and omnipotence as coping mechanisms among student psychia-trists.

The program was offered by a large university-affiliated hospital. In addition to its adult and child wards, the hospital had an active outpatient service where training cases of all degrees of severity were seen. How-ever, new residents were assigned to spend their first year on the wards, working with the hospital's most highly disturbed patients.

Most student psychiatrists came to the program with only the most rudimentary knowledge of mental illness and treatment, and they had had as yet almost no oppor-tunity to develop a sense of professional identity or a stable and reliable therapeutic stance. Yet they were expected to function as therapists for the most difficult group of patients served by the hospital, patients who predictably caused even the most experienced therapists to lose com-posure and orientation.

Many residents felt bewildered by the emotions and symptomatology they encountered on the wards. Thrust into threatening and incomprehensible circumstances, some turned to dysfunctional coping mechanisms, especially defensive distancing and omnipotence.

Over the years, I saw this process occur in a number of young psychiatrists, so that the pattern became a familiar one. Most typically, students found themselves disoriented by the neediness and rage of their patients, by their own intense reactions to the desperate personal tragedies that were constantly unfolding in their presence, and by the unrealistic expectations of co-workers.

I don't know whether the reliance on defensive omnipotence and distancing that sometimes emerged out of this convergence of inexperience and desperation persisted in all cases, but the risk seemed to be a significant one and I was never able to understand why it was necessary. If one were to purposefully seek out an environment likely to evoke dysfunctional defenses, it would be very difficult to find one more effective than the inpatient units at this facility. From a training point of view—and given the well-known dynamic relationship between feelings of helplessness and defensive omnipotence—it would have been much more useful for students to spend their most formative period under conditions that were less overwhelming.

It is likely that the practice of assigning the sickest and most difficult patients to the least experienced therapists reflected, in part, an implied devaluation of these patients. Many persons in positions of influence in the hospital believed that severely regressed patients were irredeemably damaged and unlikely to benefit from skillful therapeutic involvement. This very pessimistic orientation fostered a cycle of self-fulfilling expectations and practices. The use of beginning residents on the wards should be considered in this context.

Many residents absorbed the institutional ambience of devaluation. Some felt that their initial assignment constituted an exploitation of their relative helplessness as students—that they were being used to perform a function that more experienced staff members regarded as onerous. Many came to view their rotation on the wards as an unpleasant rite of passage. Very sick patients were resented because they were part of an ordeal that had to be undergone in order for the resident to be permitted to complete the more desirable aspects of training.

It is difficult to resist becoming socialized into an institutional consensus of devaluation and omnipotence. In addition to fitting in more comfortably with colleagues and co-workers, internalizing the consensus offers an accepted set of attitudes that help defend against threatening tensions. Thus, institutional and intrapsychic factors may support one another in generating and sustaining emotional disengagement and depersonalized interventions.

MEDICAL DOMINATION AND SPLITTING

An inherent contradiction that was becoming apparent during my years on the wards had to do with the fact that the psychiatric staff increasingly consisted of persons whose interest in mental disturbance and treatment was limited to a medical/biological dimension. Yet these same psychiatrists were invariably placed in charge of managing the psychological and interpersonal complexities of the milieu.

The contradiction was seldom openly discussed. To many, it seemed self-evident that psychiatrists should exercise ultimate authority over all aspects of practice in a psychiatric hospital. However, the suspicion that hospitals were committed to defending and preserving dysfunctional medical prerogatives was difficult to dismiss entirely, especially in the state system, where psychiatrists were least likely to be conversant in the nonbiological dimension of treatment.

In certain of the settings surveyed here, administrators were aware of the limitations of their psychiatric staff. Yet they were seldom able or willing to introduce corrective measures instituting a more rational and effective division of authority and responsibility, particularly with respect to the management of the interpersonal and psychological dimensions of milieu treatment.

Whatever their private misgivings, most administrators seemed to feel locked into the traditional form of hospital organization. Although legal and other realistic complexities were usually cited as the reason, one often had the impression that greater creativity and experimentation were possible, had the necessary determination existed.

Interdisciplinary mistrust and rivalries are likely to be exacerbated when organizational arrangements appear to be self-serving and dysfunctional, but signs of stress and strain are not necessarily visible. One typical outcome is that structural fault lines within the interdisciplinary treatment team imperceptibly widen and rigidify, and channels of communication atrophy. Primitive patients are highly attuned to the sorts of latent factional and interpersonal tensions described here and may skillfully exploit them. Thus, the team becomes more vulnerable to clinical tensions that separate staff into opposing factions, each identified with a component of primitive object relations.

When relationships among team members are significantly strained, certain vital processes are almost certain to suffer. Most obviously, it becomes extremely difficult to examine the impact patients are having on the team and on interrelationships within the team. The danger of treading dangerously close to taboo matters having to do with real struggles over power, devaluation, submission, and authority is usually too difficult to manage. The perceived threat to amicable working relations has a decisive impact in these situations. As a result, the conditions of work and interrelatedness cease to be talkable issues. Yet, it is precisely these issues that are most germane if the treatment of primitive patients is to be effective.

A dysfunctional division of authority fuels cynicism and supports defensive withdrawal from full and optimal participation. Team members find it difficult to believe in the primacy of the mission to provide treatment if the hospital appears ready to sacrifice clinical needs in order to preserve special interests.

The tendency to withdraw into hopelessness or one of its defensive transformations is especially damaging and often more complex than it appears on its surface. The affected staff person who responds in this manner to disappointing conditions of work becomes much more vulnerable to participation in and identification with the hopeless self-experience of his deeply regressed patients. This may be another example of a parallel process in which a specific hospital structure facilitates a matching primitive enactment.

Chaotic conditions and dysfunctional defensive enactments are more likely on wards where competent psychological management is lacking. Hospitals add to these conditions when they fail to organize treatment according to the realistic capacities, interests, and training of staff members. An uncritical acceptance of the medical model lends support to this unsound but widespread practice, so that to many it seems inconceivable that the division of labor, authority, and responsibility could be otherwise.

MENTAL DYSFUNCTION AS DISEASE

As noted earlier, the medical model tends to emphasize a focus on disease and this approach has made possible some of medicine's most remarkable accomplishments. However, when applied to psychiatry in a too literal fashion, the disease orientation can foster and rationalize an array of destructive attitudes and interventions.

The distinction between a person-oriented and a disease-oriented approach is central to the perspective being presented here. I must confess that I tended to regard it as mostly semantic until I had spent an extended period of time on the wards and saw for myself the truly enormous implications of treating diseases rather than working with whole persons. I have attempted to present case material in this and subsequent sections in a manner that vividly and convincingly conveys, in terms of real human lives, the ramifications of this distinction.

The disease model implies a view of mental illness as a discrete entity that in some sense resides in but is also separate from the person who has the condition. Thus, it is not difficult to believe that the illness and/or its symptoms can be treated in isolation, without having to take into account the larger human context. This is clearly an extreme version of the disease model. Yet for a variety of reasons—often having little to do with the current state of medicine or science—hospital staff members in all of the mental health professions are readily drawn into just such a stance.

Let us begin with an example, one that appears extreme but that captures a way of relating to patients that is far from unusual.

> An attractive psychotic patient who unconsciously experienced herself as a grasping monster who could never be loved was admitted to the ward after a long period of regression during which she had freely distributed sexual favors in an attempt to secure protection and caring. While on the ward, she improved in a number of respects, but persisted in offering herself to any willing male, a practice that both offended and excited members of her treatment team. The sexual behavior gradually became the central "target symptom" in her treatment, but only in terms of controlling its manifest elements. The team seemed entirely unaware of its functional significance.
>
> The patient's therapist, a man who had been raised in an authoritarian and puritanical cultural milieu, was particularly incensed about her seductiveness, in part because her behavior challenged his own sexual repressions. One day, he reported in a team meeting that he had told the patient that her promiscuity was like that of a dog. He was very proud of this intervention and felt that it would

shame the patient into more appropriate behavior. By attacking her sexuality, the therapist was attempting to establish a more comfortable distance from his own sexual needs. His anxiety was of such proportions that he could relate to her only by denying her humanity.

Mental health practitioners do things to symptoms that they would not dream of doing to human beings. Under the influence of countertransference tensions, an adversarial stance toward symptoms readily degenerates into an adversarial stance toward patients. In the case of the seductive woman, the therapist could not see the valued role her promiscuity played in maintaining some semblance of narcissistic balance, of feeling capable of inspiring love or at least interest. In attacking his patient's symptom, he was in fact attacking her self-esteem at its most vulnerable point.

The dehumanizing attack aligned the therapist's superego with sadistic superego precursors in his patient. Internally, she was attacking herself with a harsh cruelty not unlike his. At the same time, she was doing everything in her power to distance herself from self-loathing. This woman desperately needed to inspire love in order to protect herself and others from a consuming inner badness. Without realizing it, the therapist was perpetuating a defensive stance in which the patient experienced her self-loathing as deriving from the interpersonal world and acted out interpersonally—via promiscuity—in a fruitless attempt to transform it.

By defining mental symptoms as the enemy to be conquered or subdued, the medical approach contributed to this therapist's use of his regressed patient as a repository for his own hatred and feared sexual excitement. It also lent support to his superego mediated attack on her. It is depressingly easy to observe instances of these dynamics as they play themselves out on the wards. Indeed, one can discover entire wards on which an adversarial stance toward illness has become indistinguishable from feelings of hatred for patients.

Practitioners who war on disease may find it perplexing, sad, or enraging when their intended beneficiaries struggle against their best and most heart-felt efforts. It is not easy for someone trained to regard symptoms as the enemy to understand how and why deeply regressed patients so often cling to their symptoms and experience the therapy as hostile and invasive. Paradoxically, feelings of failure and frustration stemming from aggressive methods frequently lead to a greater infusion of aggression into the treatment.

Patients on wards with an adversarial orientation are often quite vocal in describing their treatment in persecutory terms. Typically, this behavior is regarded as an exacerbation of paranoid symptomatology, requiring a redoubled application of the very methods that fed into the accusations in the first place. Often in these situations, the staff employs mental health jargon as a form of obfuscation to deny the inherent aggressivity of its approach. This contributes to further clouding of reality testing.

Regressed patients need a milieu that can tolerate, contain, and channel "bad" urges, fantasies, and identifications into therapeutic relationships. Treatment methods infiltrated by hostility strengthen the cycle of projection and reintrojection of attacking part-objects, aligning the therapist with inner persecutors. Such interventions support the fear that primitive aggression cannot be safely integrated and that alienation from human connectedness is indeed irremediable.

UNILATERAL METHODS

Under the influence of the disease model, treatment tends to take on a unilateral as opposed to collaborative quality. In essence, the distinction is between "doing to" and "working with." The former is regressive in that it posits a dyad consisting of passive dependent recipient and active knowledgeable provider. The latter emphasizes shared responsibility, potential for growth, and respect for optimal autonomy.

A middle-aged woman compulsively washed her face until it was raw and bleeding. Her hospital therapist soon became frustrated by the failure of medication and redirection to have any impact on her symptom. Finally, in evident frustration, he proposed tying her hands behind her back whenever she attempted to wash her face.

Interventions of this degree of crudeness are easy to dismiss as ignorant or pathological. Yet it is remarkable how routinely one can observe instances in which staff members—in the name of treatment—aggressively attempt to take control of patients' minds, bodies, and behavior in a destructively infantilizing manner.

Many of the wards discussed here customarily employed modes of interaction that effectively confirmed their regressed patients' worst fears regarding loss of ego boundaries. On these wards, medication was routinely injected into unwilling bodies, behavior was subjected to unnecessarily harsh and arbitrary restrictions, and crude attempts were made to control unwelcome thoughts. These methods were implemented with little consideration of less aggressive alternatives and with insufficient effort to distinguish truly dangerous symptoms from those that were merely disturbing or inconvenient.

This approach is especially troubling in its failure to perceive or give sufficient weight to the potential for working together. If symptoms function in part to achieve a more secure homeostasis, it might be reasonable to assume that there is potential for collaboration between therapist and even the most regressed patient, since each is striving in his or her own way to foster greater stability. But attempts at self-regulation—especially if they are manifestly bizarre or oppositional or socially inappropriate—are too often dismissed as undifferentiated pathology or resistance. Thus, treatment readily assumes a dangerous character for the patient, because it involves a surrender of autonomy.

There is another characteristic way in which the unilateral

approach feeds into a negative therapeutic reaction. Overly zealous therapists put themselves in a position in which patients can realistically injure or defeat them by remaining ill. Patients with corrosive hatred, who envy the therapist's perceived powers, and who cannot tolerate dependency on a good object, can omnipotently triumph by "spoiling" the therapist's efforts (Rosenfeld 1964).

Feelings of demoralization and defeat are probably an inevitable consequence of working with primitive patients. Such feelings become exacerbated and malignant when the therapist is pulled into a real struggle to force the patient to become well. Under these conditions, the therapist tends to become increasingly susceptible to defensive enactments that express and ward off feelings of failure, weakness, futility, and vengefulness.

A chronically delusional middle-aged woman had been on the ward of a local state hospital for about two weeks. Because she was diabetic, her therapist ordered that urine samples were to be obtained for analysis at regular intervals.

The woman repeatedly refused to surrender her urine, but no attempt was made to understand why. After several days, the nurse in charge notified the therapist. Outraged and offended that his directive had been ignored, he ordered the nurse to catheterize the patient, if necessary by force.

Although she was not in any distress or apparent danger and despite the fact that efforts to secure her cooperation had been practically nil, the therapist did not hesitate to resort to harshly aggressive methods. He regarded the patient's insistence on retaining control of her urine as pathological, fully justifying radical invasive measures. The fact that the symptom involved a perceived challenge to his authority constituted the emotional context in which the decision to order catheterization was made.

It is almost inconceivable that a nonpsychiatric diabetic patient would be forcibly catheterized under similar circumstances. But the inability of mental patients to play an active role in their treatment is so taken for granted that they are routinely subjected to procedures that assault their bodily and psychological integrity. Mental health professionals have the widest discretion in defining and attacking what they take to be symptoms. In many instances, the aggressiveness of the attack is related more to the degree of irritation or anxiety in the staff than to the objective danger of the symptom.

In the present case, the therapist was a man who could not countenance any questioning of his authority. The patient's "challenge" to his defensive omnipotence activated underlying feelings of vulnerability and weakness. By rendering her helpless and passive, he projected and then attacked an aspect of himself that he both feared and despised. Certain components of the medical model—that he had seized upon, exaggerated, and distorted out of private anxieties—supported his readiness to see only pathology in her opposition to his wishes.

The patient's status as a person—as distinct from a disease carrier—was hardly considered as this situation developed. No one evinced the slightest interest in why she withheld her urine or in whether her refusal to cooperate might be modified by an exploration of the underlying anxiety. Even the most passing notice of her fragile ego boundaries would have suggested a graduated approach rather than one that was bound to be experienced as overwhelming. In part because of the exclusive focus on disease, it did not occur to anyone that her attempt to exercise control over her bodily functions contained an impulse toward growth and individuation. Not surprisingly, she reacted to the attempted coercion by clinging more tenaciously to the symptom that was under attack.

Unilateral disease-focused treatment does not necessarily demand that symptoms be eradicated at almost any cost, but if certain emotional ingredients are present in the clinical interaction, it readily becomes titled in that direction. Some of the most grievous injuries on psychiatric wards where I have been present over the course of many years were countertransference-based enactments of cruelty and dehumanization inflicted almost routinely by practitioners and ward staff who had persuaded themselves that they were following standard mental health procedures. The disease model—especially its adversarial stance toward symptoms and its inclination to cast the mentally ill person into the role of passive recipient—lent support to these enactments.

Fortunately, in the case of the diabetic patient, the nurse decided to ignore the catheterization order, which she considered unduly harsh and punitive. Instead, she told the patient that her cigarettes would be withheld until she provided a urine sample. The patient promptly complied and the incident, which most had regarded as unremarkable, was soon forgotten.

In contrast to the medical model, a psychoanalytic perspective emphasizes that psychological symptoms serve vital human functions, including the maintenance of homeostasis under conditions of threat. Even the most bizarre psychotic manifestations contain an impulse for survival and growth. Symptoms may be maladaptive and dysfunctional from the vantage point of external reality, but they are a key component of the patient's struggle to thrive, which is also deserving of recognition and respect.

A psychoanalytic view emphasizes the immanence of regressive and adaptive levels within every person, patient and nonpatient. This perspective has become more explicit in recent years. As the scope of analytic treatment has widened, therapists have become more willing to publish papers dealing with regressive countertransference experiences (see, for example, Boyer 1979, Giovacchini 1979, 1989, Kernberg 1987, and Searles 1965).

These writers convincingly demonstrate that a capacity for empathic identification with primitive ego states is a necessary component of clinical effectiveness; it also speaks to the commonalities of human experience. To the extent that therapists achieve a more comfortable integration of their own regressive potential, they increase their ability to work effectively with their most disturbed patients.

With this contrast in mind, it would perhaps be helpful to focus briefly on the diagnosis of mental conditions, in particular on the manner in which certain prevailing methods tend to pathologize mental patients. As usual, the impact of these methods on countertransference enactment and defense will be emphasized.

DIAGNOSIS

One of the guiding assumptions of the medical approach is that mental illness can be sorted into discrete diagnostic entities, each with its appropriate treatment, in a manner analogous to somatic conditions. This approach is exemplified most clearly in the various revisions of the *Diagnostic and Statistical Manual* of the American Psychiatric Association. The impact of this manual and of its underlying assumptions extends into all of the mental health professions and has a powerful and pervasive influence on the way mentally ill persons are experienced and treated, especially in hospital settings.

The notion that a diagnostic label can adequately capture and communicate an individual's mental and emotional dysfunction involves a remarkable diminution of human complexity. The contributors to the most recent revision of the manual (*DSM-III-R,* American Psychiatric Association, 1987) appear to recognize the inherent limitations of this methodology. They attempt to rectify it with a "multiaxial" system that permits the formulation of a composite diagnosis consisting of up to five terms. According to the revised method, patients are examined to determine possible mental disorders (Axis I), personality disorders (Axis II), physical disorders (Axis III), psychosocial stressors (Axis IV), and global assessment of functioning (Axis V). They are then assigned a label and code from each applicable axis.

Even with the multiaxial approach, *DSM-III-R* remains basically a method of assigning labels to manifest symptom clusters. For contrast, the reader might wish to examine Blanck and Blanck's process of developmental diagnosis (1974), Kernberg's method of structural diagnosis (1984), Giovacchini's classification of character structure (1975), and the diagnosis of ego functions described by Bellak and colleagues (1973). These writers seek a conceptualization of diagnosis that takes into account the complex matrix of structural, dynamic, developmental, and adaptive factors that enter into the etiology and maintenance of psychological dysfunction. Their efforts extend a tradition of ego psychology dating back to Anna Freud's work, in particular to her formulation of the multiple lines of normal and pathological development (1965).

The editor of *DSM-III-R*, Spitzer, cautions his readers against the misconception that "a classification of mental disorders classifies people, when actually what are being classified are disorders that people have. . . . [People] having the same mental disorder . . . may well differ in other important respects that may affect clinical management and outcome" (p. xxiii).

Spitzer recognizes that *DSM*-type diagnostic schemes may support the impression that people can be defined by their diagnostic label. The only way he can correct this notion is to reiterate the distinction between the disease and the person who has the disease. His need to remind users of the manual that they are dealing with human persons reflects—I believe—an understanding of the dehumanizing potential of the disease model and an attempt to shield patients from that potential.

Spitzer may be struggling with an unresolvable dilemma. In order to assert that there is more to persons than their disease, he has to insist on an artificial and untenable split between the disease and the balance of the personality. His warning reinforces a dichotomy that lies at the heart of symptom-based diagnostic systems. *DSM-III-R,* like its previous incarnations, pulls practitioners away from an observational perspective offering access to the disease as a deeply human process.

On the wards, the *DSM* approach often has precisely the impact Spitzer warns against. Bestowing a diagnosis frequently becomes an exercise in defensive distancing, dehumanization, and omnipotent control. The diagnosis is experienced as summing up an entire existence, as though the diseased individual's personhood can be dismissed or invalidated by the presence of pathology.

Deeply threatened members of the staff consolidate their defenses by clinging to an absolute distinction between those who bear a psychiatric diagnosis and those who do not—an impassable abyss separating the sick from the well. Once this context is established, countertransference-infiltrated treatment modalities and interpersonal orientations become more acceptable; a fertile soil is provided for externalization and enactment.

A schizophrenic woman in group therapy at a local hospital complained that her therapist was robbing her of her spirit. Apparently, she felt deprived of an actual inner substance that buoyed her up and without which she would sink into apathetic torpor. When questioned further, she described how the therapist responded to her complaints by patting her on the head, as though she were a child whose experience could not be taken seriously. She then pointed to a social worker in the group, a woman whom she greatly admired and envied. The therapist would never dream, she correctly observed, of patting the social worker on the head in such a fashion.

This patient was constantly being bombarded by accusatory voices that attacked and humiliated her in a manner that at times drove her to the brink of suicide. The voices expressed contempt for her sexual behavior, her craziness, her poor judgment, and so forth. She had a long history of evoking similarly hateful and contemptuous reactions in the interpersonal world. The head patting episode suggests her therapist may have permitted himself to be drawn into this process.

The therapist regarded mentally ill patients paternalistically, with a benign condescension that not infrequently served as a channel for the discharge of aggressive derivatives. His patient's status as a schizophrenic apparently relegated her to a lesser level of humanity. The presence of this diagnosis radically changed his orientation and allowed him to disguise and rationalize behavior that he would ordinarily consider patronizing.

Defining patients by their diagnosis contradicts the explicit instructions accompanying *DSM-III-R*. Why is this manual widely employed in a manner that seems oblivious to its editor's cautionary statements? In my judgment, certain of its theoretical assumptions powerfully support the modes of practice alluded to above. If mental illness is conceptualized as a discrete entity or dysfunction, afflicting diseased persons but alien to the psychological organization of well persons, and if its component processes are entirely malignant and lacking any potential to contribute to human growth and development, then these modes of practice become somewhat more understandable.

BIOLOGIZATION

Psychiatry has historically occupied a somewhat anomalous position in medicine. Because of its focus on the psyche, its development has been molded and enriched by creative tensions and cross-fertilizations between psychological and physicalistic schools of thought. In recent years, dramatic advances in the neurosciences—especially in the study of neuro-transmitters and receptors—and the impact of antipsychotic drugs have contributed to a shift in the balance in the direction of a more exclusively biological perspective.

The material to follow will touch only on certain clinical ramifications of the increasingly biological orientation of psychiatry and of the mental health professions in general. The scientific findings on which this shift is in part based will not be discussed here. Rather, I hope to alert clinicians to certain common pitfalls and misunderstandings in the application and integration of biological treatment approaches.

Psychoanalysts since Freud have recognized the role of constitutional factors in normal and pathological mental and emotional functioning. In classical metapsychology, the economic and structural points of view are the vantage points from which the impact of biology on mental development is examined. The mind is viewed as an organ that registers and regulates stimuli, particularly drives originating in the somatic system. Biologically determined differences in the intensity of drives may influence development of the mental structures. In addition, the ego itself consists in part of functional units, or "apparatuses," that follow inborn lines of development.

Kernberg (1984) provides a contemporary integrative approach that helps place the question of constitutional factors in a coherent perspective. He states that "regardless of the genetic, constitutional, biochemical, familial, psychodynamic, or psychosocial factors contributing to the etiology of the [mental/emotional] illness, the effects of all these factors are eventually reflected in the individual's psychic structure, which then becomes the underlying matrix from which behavioral symptoms develop" (p. 5).

Viewing the psychic structure as an underlying matrix can provide a framework that organizes etiological factors from disparate perspectives. It is offered here provisionally, as one example of a conceptual foundation that can support a rational, internally consistent psychotherapeutic stance with patients who need biological interventions as part of their treatment. A unifying framework helps the clinician weigh and assign an appropriate priority to treatment interventions. It also may provide guidance in sorting out countertransference elements that have distorted the treatment.

The centrality of the human personhood of the mental patient might be viewed as another such unifying framework, a concrete and palpably empirical one within which our knowledge and practice could be better considered and arranged. In the discussion to follow, a distinction is drawn between an integrated treatment approach based on respect for the encompassing human context of the regressed patient's illness and a contrasting "biologized" approach characterized by an open or implied discounting of nonneurochemical dimensions of personhood. It will be suggested that biological reductionism promotes forms of treatment that serve as channels for characteristic countertransference enactments.

MEDICATION

The reductionistic point of view can most readily be seen in the prescription and administration of psychotropic medications. The extent to which treatment is compromised by a failure to integrate drugs into a person-centered approach is immense. Even the effectiveness of the drugs themselves is undermined. Most typically, they are understood and deployed simply as weapons in the war against disease. Used in this manner, they take on powerful and destructive but largely unsuspected functions in the inner world of regressed patients and in the treatment milieu.

Primitive patients live in a world in which the parameters of existence are represented by fantasies or delusions of limitless gratification, magical soothing, and merging self and object images. They fear engulfing and devouring or being engulfed and devoured. Their vital nurturance seems in danger of being stolen, poisoned, spoiled, or transformed, precipitating panic, rage, and envy.

On many wards, these patients are confronted by a staff whose central determination (might one say passion?) is to feed or inject them with various substances intended to control their minds and bodies. The powerful regressive meanings of this interaction resonate within both staff and patients and are almost inevitably reflected in transference/countertransference dynamics. Frequently, medication comes to function as the central metaphor around which the emotions and fantasies of the milieu are organized.

It is remarkable how often treatment proceeds with little or no recognition of these powerful underlying currents. For many staff members in the facilities surveyed here, clinical investigation began and ended with identifying target symptoms and selecting an appropriate drug. The need for routine, immediate, and, if necessary, forced administration was usually regarded as self-evident. Clinicians who carefully weighed risk/benefit considerations involving medical complications often showed little awareness of psychological risk/benefit considerations.

In the state where I practiced, involuntary patients could be given medication following a commitment hearing in probate court. Although there were certain technical guidelines and limitations (for example, combining certain classes of medication was discouraged), psychiatrists and ward staff had immense discretionary authority. Patients had little alternative but to comply. To a substantial degree, their bodies and minds could be invaded and manipulated in a manner that could hardly fail to be experienced as a form of omnipotent control.

The massive imbalance of power in medication interactions functioned as a kind of magnet attracting countertransference enactments. These often involved more or less dissociated exercises in dominance and submission, retribution, or other forms of aggression, all of which were readily reinternalized to support a persecutory view of interpersonal reality.

The image of psychiatric patients as passive receptacles for medication is deeply entrenched. Routine procedures cast them in the mold of powerless and needy submissiveness. In the state hospital system, where the trend is most highly developed, even the official language reflects this orientation. For example, state patients are supposed to be referred to as "recipients." What is being proposed by this term is an image of patients as empty, helpless alimentary cavities in need of oral supplies provided by omnipotent mental health practitioners.

Both staff and patients wish to believe in the omnipotence of medication and of those who provide it. As noted by Giovacchini in the context of a discussion of antidepressant medications (1989, p. 221), therapists may be tempted to "identify with the powerful, potentially magical, curative effect" of drugs because they wish to be exalted in the same manner as the drug is exalted. On the ward, the aggrandizement of medications is pervasive and serves many needs. Even patients who fight tooth and nail against their medicine are frequently externalizing and then attacking intolerable oral dependency longings, a wish to be magically soothed and protected by omnipotent nurturers.

I have observed a number of wards where medication was given in an unconscious attempt to deny the reality of pain and suffering. These were sometimes referred to—half jokingly—as "feel good" wards, because medications were lavishly provided at the least sign of emergent distress. Many patients became psychologically addicted to the predictable and prompt soothing that was constantly being offered and had little motivation to make use of their psychotherapy. Much of what passed for treatment on these wards consisted of massive and undifferentiated gratification of regressive longings and an intensification of part-object relatedness.

Unconsciously, therapists and ward staff who use medication in this manner may be establishing themselves as idealized care-givers. The motivations are varied. Quite often, providing inappropriate gratification is meant to ward off latent narcissistic rage and other manifestations of the negative transference. The cultivation of omnipotence may also express a staff's attempt to defensively transform intolerable feelings of helplessness, futility, and depression or it may involve reparation for unconscious hatred.

Medication in Aggressive Enactments

A very paranoid young man, Mr. E., was admitted to the ward of a state hospital after becoming delusional and agitated at his mother's home. He became increasingly anxious and threatening as the time approached for his commitment hearing, as he had been told he would begin receiving medication immediately afterward.

Mr. E. had previously been given neuroleptics and experienced alarming side effects. He believed he would be permanently crippled, unable to talk properly, unable to perform his job, and unable to play his guitar if he took them again. At a deeper level, he was terribly afraid of passively submitting to what he thought were his doctor's homosexual intentions. He felt that acceptance of medication would transform him into a woman or into a weak, helpless, hungry infant. In raging against the doctor, he projected and then fought against regressive propensities that he feared and hated.

Following the commitment hearing, Mr. E. was given a long-acting injectable neuroleptic, as he refused oral medication. Because he had become threatening and agitated, several large male attendants were summoned to the ward to hold him down while the injection was being administered. When faced with this overwhelming show of force, he agreed to accept the injection. For the balance of his hospitalization, it continued to be necessary to summon help whenever the injection was due. However, when not confronted with the prospect of imminent force, the patient was calm, cooperative, and noncombative.

Gradually, Mr. E. became less delusional and more able to participate in ward activities. But he refused to believe he was being helped in any way. He continued to insist he was experiencing debilitating side effects, although only minimal signs were evident to the physician and other staff members. He also remained suspicious of his doctor's homosexual intentions.

The medication blunted certain of the psychotic symptoms that had made this hospitalization necessary. Because of his improved level of manifest functioning, it was decided that Mr. E. no longer met the criteria for involuntary treatment and he was discharged after a stay of about two months. When he left, he stated quite frankly that he might accept psychotherapy outside the hospital but would not go to the clinic for injections.

This very condensed case history illustrates a course of treatment that is very common. On one level, the young man received brief but manifestly effective treatment. As a result, he was able to resume his job and other aspects of his life that had been interrupted during the acute phase of his regression.

Yet, it is quite clear that many of Mr. E.'s most pathological tendencies had been confirmed and supported by his treatment. Even the clinicians who had provided the treatment doubted he would maintain his partial compensation for very long. They knew he had refused medication after being discharged from other hospitals and had quickly become psychotic again. Team members felt discouraged and uneasy; they believed that the patient was likely to have many subsequent readmissions in the months and years to come.

Some concluded that no truly effective intervention was possible in Mr. E.'s case, since a willingness to cooperate was clearly lacking. Others believed that the probable failure of the current approach proved the need to exercise controls more vigorously and to develop control structures that would continue to be engaged after discharge from the hospital.

Demoralization and resentment were the most prevalent reactions to treatment outcomes of this sort. Staff members were caught in a dilemma: Repeated therapeutic disappointment and frustration most typically led to a redoubling of control efforts and to an emotional orientation characterized by devaluation, emotional withdrawal, and aggression. Thus, disappointment perpetuated methods and attitudes that would probably lead to further disappointment.

There is considerably more to be learned from the case of the paranoid young man. Thus far, I have described the inadequacy of his treatment by pointing out the likelihood of continued readmissions. This sort of easily objectified criterion is useful in some respects, but it provides little help in evaluating the impact of treatment on the patient's primitive ego state and part-object relations.

Medication was the central—albeit misunderstood—metaphor in the interaction of Mr. E. with his treatment team. On the level closest to consciousness, he experienced the staff as overbearing adults who insisted that only they knew what was good for him. As a young person in his early twenties who was trying to emancipate himself from the parental orbit, the patient experienced this submission as an infantilization to be resisted. The treatment team's exaggerated focus on compliance and illness rendered it blind to the healthy maturational component in the patient's struggle.

The patient's conviction that medication would cripple him and render him unable to play his guitar was associated with fears of castration and of being transformed into a woman. Mr. E. externalized passive-homosexual longings and then combated them by attempting to defeat the suspected homosexual doctor. The doctor, unfortunately, understood this primitive defense as an interpersonal challenge, and responded by ordering a more invasive form of medication (long-acting injections) and by authorizing male attendants to hold the patient down.

The doctor and the treatment team won the power struggle, but in doing so gave the patient rather persuasive confirmation of his fear of being sadistically raped. By gratifying unconscious homosexual longings, they caused him great suffering and anxiety and placed even more strain on his tenuous ego functions. The result was an intensification of regressive defenses through which inner conflict was experienced as interpersonal.

At a still more primitive level, the patient's refusal of medication reflected a deep suspicion of nurturance. The hospital and treatment team had become associated with a feared and hated maternal part-object, a malignant and dangerous poisoner. The aggression-saturated treatment approach supported this polarized experience. The need to build trust was never recognized. The staff succeeded in force-feeding the patient, but the success was counterproductive because it exacerbated his suspicious wariness toward care-givers.

Finally, it should be apparent that the aggressive medication approach was destructive of the patient's attempts to maintain stable ego boundaries. Crudely invasive methods overwhelmed his fragile differentiation of inner and outer realities. His insistence on maintaining control of his body and mind was considered inconsequential or a manifestation of illness; what was of importance was that the team regulate his biochemical functions. The patient's use of oppositionality, paranoia, and other distancing mechanisms to ward off further blurring of self-other boundaries was intensified by this approach.

In summary, team members employed a methodology that alienated and frightened their patient, exacerbated certain of his most painful regressive tendencies, and weakened his capacity to enter into a cooperative alliance. The approach that fostered these dubious accomplishments was put into effect with little or no attempt to understand and alleviate the patient's fears or to win his partial cooperation. It was employed, not as an emergency measure, but as a fairly routine procedure for patients who refused medication, including those who were not engaging in dangerous behavior.

The treatment afforded Mr. E. was probably unnecessary, even from the perspective of symptom control. He was not initially inaccessible to a therapeutic and educative approach focused on building mutuality, cooperation, and trust. Indeed, he was able to form a constructive and gradually deepening therapeutic alliance with an activity therapist on the staff. This woman was able to reach him and enlist his collaboration in a variety of significant areas where he had initially been resistant. Had other team members exercised the same degree of skill and respect, the results of his hospitalization might have been very different.

The extent to which countertransference factors fueled aggression and dehumanization in this case cannot be known, but the clinical details certainly invite speculation. It is difficult not to question, for example, the extent to which the patient had drawn his psychiatrist into enacting the role of sadistic homosexual rapist, or whether enactments of omnipotent control had been similarly evoked. In any event, the manner in which medication was conceptualized and administered on this ward provided an inviting rationale for such enactments.

During my years on the wards, I observed hundreds of patients who showed partial or substantial alleviation of overt delusions and hallucinations in response to psychotropic medications. Yet, in a few weeks or months, many returned, often more gravely ill than before. In some cases, they had discarded their medication almost immediately. The improvements brought about by coercive or seductive unilateral interventions too often deteriorated when patients were no longer under the hospital's power and protection. Even relatively cooperative patients were frequently unable to sustain compensation when post-hospital medication was given outside the context of a secure holding relationship with a skillful therapist.

By investing medication with magical/omnipotent powers, staff members seek to distance themselves from the threatening human context of treatment. For many, belief in the omnipotence of medication constitutes the only dependable bulwark against a variety of potentially overwhelming and chaotic primitive anxieties. The absurdity of medicating symptoms while alienating the human person who experiences the symptoms may be almost impossible to recognize while these anxieties hold sway.

The current ascendancy of the biological model is widely regarded as growing entirely out of scientific advances. But it is not biological science that draws the staff to detach symptoms from their human context. Nor does biological science dictate that treatment must proceed in a manner that devalues patients' efforts to establish autonomy and secure ego boundaries. These and other equally destructive propositions turn to biology for their justification, but their origins often lie in their efficacy in warding off and/or discharging primitive countertransferences.

An Integrated Medication Approach

The effective use of psychotropic medications is far from incompatible with person-centered treatment. On a conceptual level, there is probably a consensus among mental health practitioners that the two approaches are best regarded as augmenting and enhancing one another. The interdisciplinary treatment team, with its potential integration of biological, psychological, social, and nursing perspectives is a concrete manifestation of this consensus, as is the traditional mode of psychiatric training, with its emphasis on competence in psychological and biological treatment modalities. It is on the level of day-to-day practice that the integration tends to break down.

A range of views as to the most useful conceptualization and application of biological treatment is possible under the umbrella of a person-centered approach. What is ruled out are methods that clearly undermine or devalue the human personhood of the intended beneficiary.

There are, of course, many areas of ambiguity. For example, what are we to make of the apparently ubiquitous practice of explaining to patients that they are suffering from a chemical imbalance and that medication will address and correct that imbalance? My reading of this assertion is that it overstates and oversimplifies what is actually known about the biological correlates of most mental conditions, and that it conveys an overly optimistic estimate of the effectiveness of medication treatment. Perhaps more importantly, it seems to portray the ill person—his capacity for growth and mastery and for assuming responsibility—in a distinctly diminished light. Yet, it is also true that some patients seem to derive great comfort from this way of thinking about themselves and become very anxious if it is withheld.

At the opposite end of the therapeutic spectrum lies another approach that diminishes the disturbed patient's personhood, although in a somewhat different manner. Adherents of this school of thought more or less rigidly oppose or devalue the use of medications, even in the most dire of circumstances, in the interest of protecting the technical neutrality of the treatment relationship.

This stance is not as frequently encountered in the present treatment climate as it was years ago, but despite its relatively small following, it is worth considering because it illustrates how readily the medication question can degenerate into an academic debate far removed from the actualities of real lives.

The antimedication approach begins with certain valid concerns having to do with an excessive reliance on medicine and the potential dangers of gratifying primitive incorporative needs, but it treats these concerns with little sense of context or proportion. One sometimes senses that its advocates hold doctrinal purity in higher regard than the potential seriousness of its consequences for patients.

From the standpoint of an integrated approach, questions

of context and proportion are of the essence. A clinician working in a setting such as Chestnut Lodge is able to regard medication quite differently than his counterpart in a typical state or private hospital because he can offer an intensity, duration, and sophistication of psychological treatment that is simply not feasible in most settings.

But it is not only a matter of the hospital's resources. For a variety of intrapsychic, financial, and logistical reasons, not everyone wishes or is able to undergo the long and arduous path of a Chestnut Lodge type treatment. It seems less than respectful and reasonable to strongly discourage a medication option for persons in overwhelming distress or living lives of massive functional impairment. While it is true that realistic difficulties in the path of treatment are often used in the service of resistance, they are in no way less real or less worthy of consideration for that reason.

Both schools of thought alluded to above appear to share a certain lack of seriousness. The real and vital questions of treatment integration have to do with the interrelationship of medication and psychotherapy. These issues cannot be adequately understood on the basis of rigid doctrine or oversimplification. Each unique treatment situation challenges the creativity of the clinical team to find an appropriate and effective balance, one that best suits the needs of the patient and is consistent with what the hospital can realistically offer.

My primary interest here is to indicate certain psychological considerations that can help the treatment team think more comprehensively and with a greater sense of orientation and proportion about its use of medication. What is needed is a way of discussing the impact of medication in the language of psychological constructs and processes, a sort of parallel language to supplement the usual biological and symptom-oriented formulations.

I have found it most helpful to keep in mind a model of mental development that regards psychic growth as involving the gradual mastery of various forms and degrees of anxiety.

From this perspective, using drugs to distance patients from levels of anxiety necessary for psychotherapeutic progress is seen as short-sighted. On the other hand, optimal levels of anxiety are often dangerously exceeded on the severely disturbed ward. When that happens, medicine can enhance vital capacities that threaten to become or have actually become overwhelmed.

It is important to balance the potential dangers that may result when ego functions are overwhelmed with the equally alarming dangers of iatrogenic dependency or other forms of transference/countertransference enactment. Seen in this light, the presence of symptoms is not always sufficient indication to medicate. The degree of functional impairment associated with symptoms, as well as their meaning and function within the larger psychological and therapeutic context, must also be considered.

Medications tend to be incorporated into the primitive patient's internal world of magical soothing and omnipotent care-giving. The treatment of these patients very quickly comes to focus on their demand for and struggle against unlimited oral gratifications. The provision of firm boundaries and limited gratifications is an indispensable bridge to reality. The patient's refusal to recognize the inevitability of frustration is perpetuated when medication is administered without an appreciation of its regressive pull. As a result, narcissistic rage, persecutory transformations of frustrating or alluring interpersonal objects, and retreat to hallucinatory modes of adaptation may be intensified.

These considerations suggest that questions about the use of psychotropic medications require the treatment team to know a great deal more about its patients than can be included in a diagnostic label. Viewing biological treatment as part of a larger process necessitates certain adjustments in the traditional medical model, in which correct diagnosis is the determining factor in treatment. There is frequently a good deal of anxiety and reluctance attached to making such adjustments, and not by any means only on the part of physicians. But they are of the essence if medication is to be used most effectively.

An integrated approach may require, among other things, an adjustment of priorities. For example, with oppositional patients who do not present a clear and present danger to themselves or others, it is usually more helpful to refrain from forcing medications and to concentrate instead on a psycho-therapeutic exploration of the factors interfering with the establishment of cooperation. What is usually needed is a period of preparation in which the staff comes to understand the patient in greater depth and in which a safe and empathic holding environment, fostering the growth of interpersonal trust, is established.

The cultivation of a treatment alliance with severely dis-turbed patients can be a hard task, fraught with anxieties for the patient and frequently for the therapist as well. The capacity for trust and collaboration that we tend to take for granted in our neurotic patients and that is sometimes viewed as a neces-sary precondition for successful treatment often seems to be substantially atrophied among regressed individuals. Thus, team members are often ready to dispense with efforts to provide medicine in a collaborative manner and to rely rou-tinely on unilateral methods.

The conception of treatment offered here takes a some-what different tack. It views the attainment of a more secure therapeutic alliance—capable of withstanding intensifications of primitive needs and affects—as one of the prime goals of psychotherapy with regressed patients, rather than as a precon-dition. Helping patients agree to accept medication—at least provisionally—represents a crucial landmark on the road to that goal, an initial opportunity to work together on an emo-tionally charged issue. In contrast, coercing or seducing pa-tients into greater passivity and dependence and denying them the experience of participating in a shared and responsible partnership undermines medication-induced gains.

In my experience, a substantial proportion of appropriate

candidates for psychotropic medication will, with skilled support, agree to cooperate within a few days or weeks of admission to the hospital. However, some require longer periods of preparation.

Over the years, I have worked with many individuals—both in and out of the hospital—who needed extensive psychotherapy before they were ready to consider medication. Trying to pressure compliance almost invariably produced temporary and unsatisfactory results. In contrast, providing a secure and respectful holding environment eventually made it possible for a number of extremely anxious, suspicious, and refractory patients to responsibly collaborate on a long-term basis in the medication component of their treatment. As a result, they became much more able to avoid costly and disruptive hospitalizations than if they had been coercively medicated in the manner described earlier in this chapter.

I sometimes find it conceptually useful to artificially divide my work with medication patients into two very inexact and overlapping categories. Each of these modes offers interesting challenges and the satisfaction of contributing to areas of potential psychological growth.

In the first, the therapeutic relationship is viewed as a means of helping patients become more willing and responsible collaborators in their medication regimen. This way of working is intended in part to support the psychiatrist's efforts, but it is not strictly necessary to regard it as an ancillary function. Helping to establish a secure holding environment and an embryonic therapeutic alliance contribute independently to the patient's recovery and development, in addition to whatever role they play in facilitating acceptance of medicine. Indeed, with some patients, what begins as a facilitating effort evolves over time into the central focus of working together.

In the second category, the medicine is regarded as a means of helping acutely disturbed patients become more accessible to psychotherapy. There is an assumption here that the patient will be able to make substantial use of the therapy when the acute disturbance has been ameliorated, but not necessarily that the medication will become unneeded at that point.

It is difficult to make hard and fast rules as to what is ancillary and what is primary in an integrated approach. The work of treatment team members is so intertwined and interdependent that such distinctions often have little clinical meaning. What is clear is that successful teams are characterized by mutual respect and recognition of areas of special expertise among teammates. In such teams, the psychologist serves as a consultant for the biologically oriented psychiatrist and vice versa. There are probably a number of ways in which the team may be organized to provide effective leadership and coordination, but an integrated approach requires an alteration of the automatic presumption that the psychiatrist is necessarily best suited to oversee all components of the treatment.

An additional note of caution is in order. To suggest to a highly anxious staff that it precipitously sacrifice immediate symptom control in the interest of cultivating collaborative treatment relationships is likely to be experienced by many as the equivalent of being deprived of a life preserver. As will be noted in greater detail in the discussion of nursing (Chapter 3) and the treatment team (Chapter 4), a staff often requires long periods of preparatory work before it is able to provide an effective holding environment in which medication use is guided by the considerations discussed here. Wards where medication functions as a pillar of countertransference defense and enactment are, at best, very slow to change.

In this section, I have attempted to illustrate how the medical view of mental illness and treatment, or at least a certain version of it, supports a variety of destructive countertransference enactments. The medical model serves as a conceptual basis for treatment within most psychiatric settings and has a substantial impact on all the mental health disciplines. Its potential for misuse as a countertransference structure has, in my view, not been sufficiently considered.

3

Nursing

The ward milieu is an exquisitely sensitive instrument, registering and reacting to the most subtle of nuances. At its best, it contains and therapeutically processes deeply disturbing impulses, fears, fantasy, and behavior. The dynamics of the milieu are shaped by constant tensions between the need for expression and security. These tensions can be continually rediscovered in fresh clinical material. If used creatively, they can help patients and staff understand and modify their inner states and interrelationships.

In office practice, therapists attempt to cope with the constantly shifting manifestations of transference and counter-transference within a dyad. In an institutional setting, the problem becomes vastly more complex. For one thing, the transferences tend to be a great deal more disturbing than those ordinarily seen in office practice. And in addition to managing their own reactions, therapists must interact in an educational and psychologically supportive manner with co-workers who are also drawn into the transference/countertransference matrix.

The ward milieu is a primary arena in which primitive internalized object relations are lived out and reintrojected. Efforts to interrupt and rechannel enactments are every bit as crucial as ongoing dyadic therapy. But working with the milieu evokes stubborn resistances, many of which are supported by institutional arrangements. These arrangements undermine treatment by interfering with the milieu's receptive and containment functions.

THE SPECIAL ROLE OF NURSES IN WARD DYNAMICS

In my work on the wards, I soon became aware of the pivotal role of nursing staff (unless otherwise noted, the term will be used inclusively to refer to registered nurses, practical nurses, and nursing aides). It was clear that nurses were frequently at the center of crucial transference/countertransference constellations. Yet, they tended to see themselves and to be seen by co-workers and administrators as attending mainly to the practical aspects of managing the ward.

How is the fact that nurses are often at the center of activated psychological tensions so frequently overlooked? In part, it can be understood as a form of psychogenic myopia, owing much to the power of anxiety. In addition, it tends to be supported by entrenched institutional arrangements.

Bringing the primitive transferences that reverberate around nurses out of the realm of enactment and into the treatment process requires bringing nurses into more active clinical participation. However, many individuals and groups within the hospital—including nurses themselves—tend to oppose efforts to reconceptualize and restructure traditional nursing roles.

Working with and through nurses represents a unique

opportunity to reach patients at a meaningful level. But nurses have special needs, vulnerabilities, and areas of stress that have to be understood and addressed if they are to become effective agents of therapeutic change.

The context in which nurses relate to patients is especially stressful. The other professional disciplines interact with patients mostly through scheduled or otherwise circumscribed activities. These are usually limited in time, have a clearly defined purpose, and are conducted on a relatively de-instinctualized plane. This helps to tone down primitive impulses and channel them into manageable forms of expression.

Nurses, however, have a much less structured, less predictable, and more impulse-ridden context in which to work. They are available throughout their shifts and are expected to respond immediately to any contingency, including situations that evoke intense feelings of fear, hatred, disgust, or excitement. Nurses provide a continual presence on the wards. Most do not have the opportunity to spend large blocks of time in off-ward offices where they can physically and emotionally regroup.

Because they provide hands-on interventions involving maternal functions, such as attending to basic physical and emotional needs, nurses are likely to become the targets of demands for unlimited caretaking and oral supplies, as well as for narcissistic rage when demands are not met. When patients lose control, nurses administer emergency medications and physical management, serving as the behavior controllers of last resort.

As care-givers and limit-setters, nurses are especially likely to be experienced as hateful persecutors or idealized nurturers and to be drawn into enactments of one or another of these part-object identifications. Helping them tolerate and make clinical use of the powerful regressive forces bound up with their realistic functions is thus a vital task.

But this task must be approached cautiously. Bringing nurses into more active clinical participation risks exacerbating certain deeply entrenched resistances. Two are especially worth noting: The first has to do with the heightened dangers nurses fear they will encounter in an expressive treatment milieu; the second involves the devalued position of nurses in many hospital hierarchies. Each of these difficulties is associated with characteristic defensive enactments and disruptive tensions within the treatment team. In the material to follow, these complications will be discussed in some detail.

NURSES IN THE EXPRESSIVE MILIEU

Nurses tend to be suspicious of efforts to encourage expressivity, especially on wards where potentially dangerous or disruptive patients are treated. This resistance, based as it is upon some degree of reality, is deeply ingrained and requires very patient work if nurses are to be convinced of the merits of an expressive approach.

When I began my work on the wards, I was surprised to see how frequently nurses overtly and covertly worked against my efforts to teach and practice expressive therapy. It did not take long to discover that they feared increased toleration would inevitably lead to chaos. Although this fear was not unique to nurses, as a group they had the most to lose from uncontrolled acting out, even to the extent of risking personal injury to restore order.

No attempt to enlist the cooperation of nurses can be successful if it is not based on a realistic understanding of how they perceive their self-interest. Although safety and control issues often link up with countertransference tensions, treating these concerns as if they represent personal pathology is a major blunder. Nurses will invariably do what they think is necessary to increase a sense of security. An expressive milieu cannot be established or maintained until the staff comes to understand that it can provide more rather than less security.

Attempts to mandate threatening changes are invariably met with sabotage, alienation, or disregard.

Tensions between the need for expression and the need for containment are inevitable in any setting where severely disturbed individuals are treated. In part, this reflects the externalization of an inner tension. To help patients work toward a more integrated and modulated level of functioning, it is necessary that staff members refrain from identifying with and enacting opposing sides of primitive intrapsychic struggles. Conflicts between nurses and other factions of the staff sustain defensive splits within patients. Thus, resolving disagreements over expressivity and control lies at the very heart of milieu treatment.

Most nurses are not unalterably committed to the belief that a tolerant expressive milieu is inimical to their safety and well-being. In order to enlist and maintain their support, it is necessary that the clinician never minimize the anxieties that are continually activated by the flaring up of psychotic processes. Most importantly, the milieu must develop structures into which activated tensions can be safely and productively channeled and contained.

The clinician can help nurses gradually replace infantilizing control mechanisms with forms of therapeutic containment that permit modulated—especially verbal—expression of primitive processes. In the course of case discussions with the staff, it often becomes apparent that resistances to expressivity are associated with specific anxiety-laden elements of the clinical material. These can become workable if the clinician fosters a trusting and nonpunitive relationship with staff and is willing to forego immediate change when anxieties are too intense. Chapter 4 illustrates in some detail how team processes contribute to this shift in the functioning of the milieu.

For now, it will only be noted that the phrase "working with nurses" refers to a process in which the clinician helps teammates disengage from various forms of reflexive enactment, in particular the infiltration of nursing interventions by derivatives of dehumanization, splitting, omnipotent control, and idealization. Nurses are helped to utilize their receptive capacities in a less defensive mode and to tolerate and contain the feelings and fantasies triggered by their patients. In this manner, ordinary nursing interactions can become a potent component of milieu treatment.

DEVALUATION OF NURSES

Nurses in the psychiatic hospital examined here typically occupied the bottom rung of the medical hierarchy. Their relations with administrators tended to be more adversarial and less collegial than was the case with other professional staff. In some settings, relations periodically deteriorated into more or less open warfare in the form of labor-management disputes that left each side embittered and alienated.

Institutional arrangements that devalue nurses contribute to a climate in which nurses are more likely to be used as repositories for patients' split-off bad internal contents. They also contribute to aggressive acting out via nursing interventions, a form of identification with the aggressor. As this chapter proceeds, examples of each will be provided and discussed.

Disciplinary Policies

Mistrustful hierarchical relations between nurses and administrators can be seen clearly in the disciplinary procedures of certain hospitals, especially in the state system. These legalistic and punitive measures—intended to protect patients from abuse and neglect—not only devalued nurses, who were seen as the most likely offenders, but they infused the treatment milieu with an additional source of interdisciplinary suspiciousness and resentful acting out. Patients frequently were close observers of these relations among their caretakers and saw in them confirmation of aggression-laden internal object relations.

It may be helpful now to explore in some detail the clinical impact of adversarial disciplinary policies in a hospital where fault-finding, punishment, and atrophied lines of communication were a significant component of relations between nurses and administrators. Unresolved conflict between nurses and administration disrupted clinical processes by fueling mistrust among members of the interdisciplinary treatment team and by adding to the potential for aggression and devaluation in the milieu.

At the hospital in question—referred to here as Midtown Psychiatric Center—registered nurses were a minority in the nursing department and occupied mostly supervisory positions. The bulk of nursing consisted of licensed practical nurses (LPNs) and nursing aides (NAs).

Attempts to work clinically with nurses at MPC were complicated by a long history of punitive and devaluing personnel practices. It was a common occurrence for nurses to be punished or embarrassed in a clumsy and heavy-handed manner for relatively minor errors or procedural infractions. I saw ample evidence of how this approach demoralized the staff and injected bitterness and resentment into the milieu. Nurses who might otherwise have become full and active participants in the team grew mistrustful and withdrawn, going through the motions of participation in a team effort but not really giving of themselves.

Disciplinary procedures at MPC operated with far too little discrimination between intentional infractions and more benign mistakes of judgment, and with little flexibility as to whether punitive measures might best be tempered in certain circumstances or with certain individuals. This approach was inherently devaluing because it assumed nurses did not have personal and professional ideals, that they could be motivated only by punishment. But despite its harshness and rigidity, the process was remarkably ineffective in dealing with individuals who had been guilty of willful and serious acts of abuse and/or neglect.

To work effectively on countertransference issues in the milieu, it was necessary to come to grips with the resentment and mistrust that was an inevitable by-product of the hospital's punitive approach. To begin with, it was crucial to provide a climate in which nurses could talk freely about their interactions with patients without fear of disciplinary action or embarrassment. The degree of protection and confidentiality could not be unlimited, but a fairly wide discretion was needed. This approach required of the clinician, at least in certain cases, a willingness to assume personal responsibility for dealing with errors and infractions, in effect bypassing the hospital's formal punitive structures.

Taking a clinical and educational approach was a subject of anxiety because it entailed circumventing policies that were intended to protect patients from abuse and neglect, policies that allowed little room for discretion. Adding to the anxiety was the fact that it was impossible to know unambiguously in each case that the benefits outweighed the risks.

However, working with errors involved something far more important than the relative effectiveness or ineffectiveness of the disciplinary system. The hospital's view was that errors were to be regarded as infractions and dealt with accordingly. This was untenable. From a clinical perspective, these infractions often represented activated externalizations of primitive psychological states. *Understanding and working with enactments constituted a sort of royal road into the milieu's dynamic unconscious.* Nurses, who were at the very heart of activated tensions, had to be enlisted in the process if it was to have any chance of succeeding.

Working with nursing staff involves creating an environment in which countertransference-based errors can be safely examined, facilitating an eventual shift to a more sophisticated mode of interacting. At MPC, many errors were relatively petty, but would nevertheless have elicited punitive measures if handled through normal supervisory channels. It was easy to decide to bypass the disciplinary process when the infraction was slight and the potential for harm from the anticipated bureaucratic overkill was great. Occasionally, however, situations occurred in which choosing a course of action was a good deal more perplexing.

The example to follow falls into the latter category. It involves an incident in which I observed a nursing aide physically attack a psychotic patient. I will attempt to describe the dilemma I faced in dealing with what I had witnessed.

The patient was a man whom I had treated during the course of numerous hospitalizations. He typically was very psychotic on admission, but responded to treatment within a few weeks and was able to reach a level of functioning in which no overt psychotic process was evident.

The patient was known for his habit of constantly carrying a paper cup and spitting into it from time to time with great disgust. During an earlier admission, I had finally succeeded in talking with him about the cup and discovered that for many years he had been hallucinating a penis ejaculating into his mouth. We then had a number of sessions in which we talked about certain homosexual concerns he had previously been too anxious to mention.

What developed out of this work was that the patient's chronic homosexual anxiety was somewhat alleviated and he became able to rely on higher level defenses. He became quite an amusing flirt with the women on the ward and was pugnacious toward the men. His flirtatiousness and his masculine swaggering had a playful and exaggerated quality, so that his behavior was never experienced as cause for alarm.

The aide, Mr. V., was a man who had worked at MPC for a number of years. He had always been rather quiet and reserved, but was generally considered to be reliable and conscientious. I knew him to be capable of making astute observations about the patients and the milieu, although it was true that he too often kept his thoughts to himself. In the weeks prior to the incident in question, Mr. V. had seemed more morose than usual. Without really taking note of it, I had been making an effort to leave him alone, as I sensed he did not want to be intruded upon. I think it was clear to most of the staff during those weeks that Mr. V. was experiencing unusual stress and that his controls were frayed, but as far as I know, no one attempted to talk to him about it.

The incident in question lasted only a few seconds. The psychotic patient, as was his custom from time to time, had been harassing and verbally abusing Mr. V. in the hallway of the ward. Evidently, he had miscalculated how far he could go. When I came upon the scene, Mr. V. was striking the patient on the chest with his open palms, pushing him toward the wall. He was a powerfully built man and was clearly very angry. The situation might well have escalated further if I had not appeared. At any rate, Mr. V. saw me and abruptly stopped and walked away. The patient, whose braggadocio had abandoned him for a few moments, saw that he was now safe and sent Mr. V. on his way with a few more choice bits of abuse.

From the standpoint of countertransference acting out, the interaction I had chanced to witness was fairly comprehensible. The patient had succeeded in activating hostility in an individual who was especially vulnerable. The aide had been drawn into colluding in a defensive posture in which wishes for homosexual closeness were transformed into apparent hostility, in the manner described in Freud's classic formulation. Perhaps there had been gratification of the patient's underlying homosexual wish in the physical contact that was evoked.

However, from the standpoint of having to decide how to deal with it, the incident was far from comprehensible. The mandate to report abusive behavior was unambiguous and left no room for clinical discretion. Yet I was troubled by the fact that Mr. V.'s behavior was so unlike his usual quiet and patient way of responding to provocative patients.

In addition, I had little confidence in the hospital's ability to deal with this incident in a helpful and constructive manner. I knew that if Mr. V. was reported, the disciplinary process that was certain to follow would take place on an adversarial level and that the result would be punitive, humiliating, and likely to embitter an individual who clearly had the capacity to make a valuable contribution to the ward.

But regardless of my assessment of Mr. V. and of the disciplinary system, my primary duty was to protect patients from abuse. According to the logic of the hospital, an individual who had lost control could not go unpunished. If I failed to report him, I would be neglecting my duty to help provide patients with a reasonably safe environment.

These were some of the thoughts that were swirling in my mind as I attempted to regain my composure. On the way back to my office, where I planned to sit and think for a while, I stepped into the nursing station. The charge nurse that afternoon was an older woman whom I had known since I joined the staff several years earlier. She had always been very kind to me and was a person whose judgment and experience I had grown to depend on. Although I had thought I would not say anything about the incident until I had carefully weighed the alternatives, I impulsively confided in her that I had just seen Mr. V. strike a patient and that I thought he might well be in serious trouble.

The nurse may have told Mr. V. what I said to her. At any rate, he knocked on my office door a few minutes later and asked if we could talk. Our conversation lasted about 30 minutes. Mostly, we spoke about the patient and why he needed to provoke hostility in Mr. V. I mentioned that I had found him rather tense in recent weeks and that the patient may have made the most of his bad mood. He did not volunteer much information about what was upsetting him but I had the impression it had to do with family difficulties.

In retrospect, I can see that I was using our meeting to try to decide more clearly what I thought about Mr. V.'s reaction to what had transpired on the ward and, in more general terms, to form a clearer opinion about his character. I wanted to know to what degree he experienced his loss of control as ego-dystonic and whether he had been sufficiently shaken by it to make certain that he got a tighter grip on himself. Or was he merely trying to ingratiate himself with me so that I would not report the incident.

In the end, I decided to keep silent and to see how the situation developed. My reasons were as follows: I believed that Mr. V.'s loss of control was an isolated occurrence and that he was a basically conscientious person who had been shocked and surprised by his own actions. Referring the matter for discipline seemed unnecessary from the point of view of ward safety and counterproductive in terms of its probable impact on Mr. V.

I would like now to examine this dilemma from the perspective of Mr. V.'s functioning on the ward in the months and years that followed this incident. For the next few weeks, he regarded me rather warily, as if waiting for the axe to fall. Gradually, though, he began to seem more at ease about my intentions. As the months passed, his mood of tense preoccupation gradually lifted. Perhaps what had been troubling him had been resolved. At any rate, Mr. V. was once again the quiet but competent and approachable person he had been before.

I noticed, however, that he now seemed to be taking a more active interest in team meetings and showing greater curiosity about dynamic issues in the milieu. Increasingly, I found him supportive and understanding when the ward was stirred up by conflict and tension. During this same period of time, I increasingly heard reports from patients of Mr. V.'s helpful and sensitive involvement. It seemed clear that he was becoming a person who played an important role in the treatment effort.

This involvement became most evident about two years later, during a period when the ward was going through a great deal of turmoil marked by intense splitting of the staff. We had on the ward at that time a manic woman who was capable of creating almost unbelievable havoc and polarization in her environment. Not only was she psychologically disturbing, she was also physically dangerous. Her year on the ward was easily one of the most trying periods of my career at MPC.

During that year, Mr. V. was the only member of the nursing staff who succeeded in establishing a relationship with this patient. He sat with her quietly day after day, gradually winning her confidence, sharing her interests, and allowing her to use him as a bridge to more widespread participation in the milieu. In order to accomplish this, he had to weather the patient's scorn, contempt, and provocations for many weeks and months. He made this truly skillful and emotionally demanding effort on his own volition. His supervisors and co-workers had distanced themselves from the patient and were surprised he had not done the same.

I have presented this case at some length because of its intrinsic interest and also because it illustrates the outer limits of my policy of bypassing the disciplinary system at MPC. I recognize that there were substantial risks and that some readers may consider my actions ill advised. In my defense, I can only say that I felt impelled to weigh the limitations of my ability to assess Mr. V. and predict his behavior against the disciplinary system's unambiguous destructiveness and ineffectuality. As I continue to add details of the psychological climate and policy arrangements at MPC, I hope the reasons for my decision will seem more understandable.

The effectiveness of the MPC disciplinary system in containing the volatility of the treatment milieu was seriously compromised by unresolved tensions in the relationship between nursing and the hospital administration. So many aspects of the relationship were colored by mistrust, devaluation, and the perception of opposing interests that it is perhaps not surprising that the process of rooting out chronic abusers was experienced by many as anti-nursing, pitting management against labor, rather than as a cooperative effort in which both sides might join forces.

The disciplinary system took little cognizance of the unique pressures faced by nurses who had to provide hands-on interventions under the most extreme circumstances. When all else failed, it was their job to restore some semblance of order and control to the milieu. This not infrequently required the use of physical or chemical restraint. Nurses who performed these functions were under immense stress. Not only were they in danger of being injured, but they were quite aware that hospital administrators were likely to subject the incident to a legalistic and adversarial post hoc examination.

The MPC disciplinary process, with its incredibly cumbersome and rigid welter of regulations, investigations, punishments, and appeals can be seen as a prototypical example of a countertherapeutic institutional structure. Probably, the convolutions built into the system were considered necessary for the protection of due process. However, safeguards had become so dense and cumbersome as to make it very difficult to protect patients from chronic abusers.

Even the most seemingly simple and straightforward disciplinary action might be countered with grievance claims that would keep the matter tied up in a succession of hearings for many months, during which time the staff person involved would continue to work in close contact with patients. After the torturously ponderous process had been completed, the resolution was seldom satisfactory. It typically took many years and a series of successfully prosecuted disciplinary actions—each followed by a relatively ineffectual punishment—before a seriously abusive employee could finally be terminated.

The inertia and ineffectuality was extremely discouraging and demoralizing to administrators, therapists, and nurses. For some, discouragement led to cynicism or paralysis. I personally knew any number of nurses who kept silent or otherwise refused to become involved in efforts to deal with abusive employees because of a conviction that such efforts would not lead to definitive changes or might even be counterproductive.

The nurses' labor union vigorously defended members accused of abuse or neglect, even in instances in which the facts of the case were seemingly beyond dispute. Many union members with whom I discussed this situation were embarrassed and dismayed, yet they felt a need to maintain solidarity against procedures that were perceived as anti-nursing. Regardless of the feelings of individual nurses, on an organizational level the dynamics of adversarial relationships held sway.

I recall one instance in which I had been called to testify at a hearing involving a staff person who had, over the years, been repeatedly embroiled in incidents of neglect and insubordination. Despite the fact that virtually everyone in the hospital was acquainted with this person's refusal to perform his duties, the union official who represented him turned the hearing into an attack on the hospital. When my turn came to testify regarding the incident I had witnessed, the official subjected me to a bombardment of abuse and innuendo.

The atmosphere that prevailed at this hearing was fairly typical and illustrates the extent to which the hospital and its employees had failed to define a sense of common purpose. In this particular instance, the employee returned to his job after having received a mostly symbolic slap on the wrist, convinced as ever that he could conduct himself however he might choose.

In the years that followed, he continued to defy routine instructions, even neglecting to give patients needed medical care. I remember one instance in which he refused to give medication to a patient who was experiencing severe extrapyramidal symptoms, apparently because he was feuding with a supervisor.

This employee was an extremely hostile and litigious individual who experienced himself as locked in battle with enemies attempting to degrade and humiliate him. The very real conflict between nurses and administration did little to disabuse him of these notions. Although he did not, to my knowledge, physically abuse patients, his attitude was at best castrating and devaluing and he clearly had no business working with vulnerable mental patients. Yet, the union aggressively protected him, making it impossible to either help him or get rid of him. As a result, he made his presence felt in repeated incidents of the sort described above, creating conflict and dissension on every ward to which he was assigned.

In terms of overt physical abuse, however, there were persons on our staff who were far more dangerous. As a therapist, I heard all sorts of reports and complaints of abuse from my patients. Over the years, I noted that certain staff members were almost never mentioned whereas others were regularly identified as perpetrators. When I compared notes with colleagues, it was clear that their experience was similar to mine. The picture that emerged was of a small core of individuals who apparently were guilty of the great preponderance of serious intentional abuse and gross neglect.

The hospital administration and the Department of Nursing were also aware of the identities and activities of certain of these staff members because they tended to be repeatedly named in off-the-record conversations with clinicians and nursing supervisors. Yet, the disciplinary process was often ineffectual in protecting our patients from them.

One of the great difficulties in removing them was that it was often very difficult to satisfy the standards of proof demanded by the disciplinary system. Since so many of the hospital's patients were delusional, it was relatively easy to convince a hearings officer that accusations were the product of a patient's imagination, especially when no witnesses had been present. Certain predatory members of the staff were well aware of and took advantage of this state of affairs. Patients knew they had little credibility and often declined to make formal complaints.

A very depressed young woman who desperately wanted to leave the hospital in order to see her young children was told by a NA that he would leave a door ajar so that she could escape if she would have sex with him. The patient agreed and the NA took her to a secluded area during an off-ward recreation period. Later, however, she found that the designated door was locked as usual. When she confronted the NA, he simply laughed at her and claimed not to know what she was talking about. In this case, the patient was unwilling to make a complaint, in part because of her complicity in the matter, but also because she was aware that, as a patient, her word carried little weight.

Filing complaints might also bring on further intimidation. Patients knew they were tremendously dependent on the good will of those who cared for them. Even implied intimidation from staff members endowed with such disproportionate power could be tremendously effective in inhibiting complaints.

To prevent intimidation, staff members who had been accused of abuse were supposed to be transferred to another ward while the complaint was being investigated. However, this mechanism was easily circumvented.

A NA who had been reassigned after a complaint of abuse appeared on his original ward during break periods, ostensibly to chat with a co-worker. These visits continued over several days. The NA circulated fairly freely, making a point of saying a few words to the patient who filed the complaint, so that it became obvious that the safety he had been promised could not be depended upon. The NA gained access to the ward because nurses there were willing to look the other way rather than appear to align themselves with a disciplinary procedure they experienced as demeaning.

Intimidation was not limited to implied threats. I knew of one member of our staff who had, over the years, repeatedly and intentionally used physical abuse to intimidate patients, but only when he was alone with them or when he was confident that any co-workers who were present would not report him. He would threaten to administer an even more severe beating if the patient complained about him. I saw the results of one of these beatings, but I was unable to persuade the patient to talk to an investigator or file a complaint. If patients repeated the perpetrator's explanation of the injury, the hospital had no alternative but to accept that version.

Therapists, nurses, and administrators knew there were chronic and/or opportunistic abusers on the staff and had a fairly reliable idea who they were. But there too often seemed little anyone could do about them; they were securely lodged in the system. Clearly, had there been a more conciliatory and mutually respectful relationship between nurses and administration, the problem might have been dealt with a good deal more effectively.

It would be unfair not to acknowledge that personnel

relations at MPC evolved in part out of an array of social, economic, and historical conditions over which persons in the hospital had little or no control. However, it is also worth noting that hardly anyone at MPC recognized the seriousness of alienation among nurses, especially its impact on all aspects of milieu treatment. In large measure, this was due to the hospital's frame of reference. According to customary parlance at MPC, only psychiatrists, psychologists, and social workers were recognized as clinical staff. Clinical staff engaged in treatment-related activities whereas nurses assisted with tasks of a lesser significance. This mostly unexamined assumption had much to do with the fact that little concerted effort was made to draw nurses into a more active and mutually respectful clinical partnership.

A related impediment was the widespread tendency to misunderstand the nature of abuse and other forms of mistreatment. Mistreatment is usually best understood not as an infraction, but as a form of enactment, and as such implies a certain readiness or personal predisposition on the part of the enactor. Thus, a continuum might be said to exist between staff members who are very ready to act out and those who act out only under conditions of considerable tension and provocation. It is crucial both for treatment and for staff morale to distinguish between persons who fall at different ends of this continuum. A hospital should be free to act decisively to remove truly dangerous and otherwise unsuitable persons from positions in which they can do harm. But it is clearly counterproductive to treat the great preponderance of well-intentioned staff members in the same punitive mode.

I observed very substantial changes in staff interrelationships and efffectiveness when I was able to handle errors in a manner that presupposed the possibility of a respectful clinical partnership. As I noted in the case of the nursing aide, Mr. V., this sometimes meant working outside of the hospital's disciplinary system. Chapter 4 describes in detail a method of reducing destructive enactments by helping staff members channel milieu tensions into a team structure capable of receiving, working over, and containing primitive projections.

The approach I am outlining here is far from new or radical. It represents a distillation of a model of clinical learning that is inherent in the training of psychotherapists. It can be seen clearly in clinical supervision when trust and collaboration develop to a degree that permits an in-depth exploration of errors. This approach is based on respect for the student's seriousness of purpose and an avoidance of methods that foster regressive interpersonal relations.

NURSES AS REPOSITORIES FOR BAD INTERNAL CONTENTS

Primitive patients make use of whatever is available in the interpersonal environment in order to bolster defensive needs. Consistent with their persecutory and grandiose preoccupations, they seem specially attuned to the distribution of status and authority among hospital staff members. If one group appears to be undervalued and subject to attack, its members may become an inviting target for projections of despised and feared internal self and object components. Psychiatric nurses at MPC, who invariably had the dirtiest and most dangerous jobs, who received but seldom gave instructions, and whose at times truly heroic efforts to provide skillful and compassionate care were seldom recognized, were prime candidates for these projections.

Devaluing status hierarchies disrupt milieu treatment by supporting enactments of splitting, omnipotence, and dehumanization. At MPC, a factor that further complicated the task of working with the impact of devaluation was the racial composition of the wards. Most patients and nursing staff were black, while most of the psychiatrists, social workers, and psychologists were white. Among patients, identifying blackness as the color of shameful and degraded internal contents and whiteness as the hallmark of perfection, power, and goodness was not unusual. The devalued status of the mostly black nursing staff supported this internal polarization and the unconscious anxieties on which it was based.

These feelings were usually played out more or less quietly in the course of innumerable interpersonal interactions that, in their cumulative impact, contributed to an awkward tension that staff members found difficult to discuss comfortably, at least across racial lines.

At times, however, they were played out more publicly. For example, in ward community meetings black patients would occasionally deliver harangues attacking the filthy, vicious, immoral, or greedy blacks. Often, they would point out nurses in the meetings as prime examples of these qualities.

The targets of these primitive attacks frequently seemed unable to respond as effectively as one might have expected. In part, this stemmed from an acute awareness of their realistically devalued status within the hospital. Patients very skillfully used and distorted this vulnerability to rationalize and justify their attacks.

In Chapter 1, I referred in some detail to a paper by Kernberg (1987) in which he noted splits along racial lines that supported the projection of primitive part-objects. The more a staff is realistically factionalized, the more difficult it becomes to recognize and cope therapeutically with those elements that have been introjected from patients.

DEVALUATION AND SPLITTING

Several years ago, I became aware of an apparently unsolvable situation that was poisoning relationships and paralyzing treatment efforts on a ward where one of my students was assigned. A borderline patient had succeeded in polarizing the treatment team so that nurses were bitterly pitted against the patient's therapist. Each side in this dispute was actively undermining the efforts of the other. The situation had deteriorated to such an extent that the patient was able to provoke both the nurses and the therapist into making openly derogatory comments about one another.

The situation developed in the following manner: The therapist was known for his blunt and sarcastic manner of expressing dissatisfaction with the quality of nursing care at MPC. These criticisms contained realistic elements, but also served as a thinly veiled rationalization for his rather global contempt for nurses. The borderline patient quickly noticed that the therapist was highly sympathetic to his complaints of being mistreated. Soon, he enlisted the therapist's help in providing protection from the "acting out" of the nurses.

The therapist, who needed and enjoyed his status as an idealized rescuer, was always ready to intervene to save the patient from the incompetent, cruel, and uncaring nurses. The nurses, for their part, were furious with him for casting them in the role of villains and for coddling the patient. Their anger and sense of impotence sometimes led them to lash out aggressively against the patient, thus reinvigorating the cycle of splitting, projection, and reintrojection.

Eventually, tensions reached such a pitch that an angry confrontation took place between the nursing staff and my student, who was regarded as the therapist's representative. The therapist did not attend the meeting in which this confrontation took place. In part, this was due to his having pressing responsibilities elsewhere in the hospital. However, his absence also reflected a wish to distance himself from nursing and milieu issues by dealing with them through the student.

The student slowly grasped the meaning of the split, including her participation in facilitating the separation. But the therapist continued to avoid direct participation. He would come to the ward only to meet briefly with patients or to write notes in the chart. The student meanwhile engaged in a sort of shuttle diplomacy, attempting to diffuse anger and misunderstandings but unable to bring the sides together for a prolonged period of work. Although her efforts somewhat moderated the resentment and acting out, both sides continued to be committed to antagonistic and devaluing views of one another, and this alienation was more or less exploited by the borderline patient for a long period of time.

The devaluation of nurses may be so seamlessly integrated into a hospital's collective consciousness that it is virtually unnoticed until a crisis occurs. Then, resentments may become manifest in ways that seem shocking and out of proportion. Consider, for example, the developments surrounding the hospital stay of a dangerous and severely paranoid man, Mr. F.

Mr. F. blamed doctors for his mother's death and was convinced they meant to kill him too. Shortly after being admitted to a state hospital, he attacked and injured his therapist. The beating was serious and the therapist was no longer able to work with Mr. F., especially as the patient was promising to attack him again at the first opportunity.

The patient was transferred to a second therapist, who also experienced immense difficulties. The patient told him he could appeal to powerful supernatural forces who would grant him power to gain a bloody revenge on those persons who were tormenting him and his family. The new therapist decided to keep the patient in restraints, because he believed he would explode again at any moment.

Because of the turmoil and anxiety evoked by this case, it was eventually decided that a well-known local consultant would be asked to assist the treatment team. The initial conference was attended by a larger than usual group because of the notoriety of the circumstances. Almost immediately, a nursing aide interrupted the orderly presentation of case material and began a furious denunciation of staff members who—in his view—typically ran away instead of helping nurses who were endangered by violent patients. The NA was clearly outraged. He began to give details of the serious injuries incurred by nurses and accused therapists and social workers of hiding in their offices whenever patients were out of control.

The other participants sat in silence while the usual rules of decorum were violated. The NA even shouted down the distinguished consultant, who tried to reason with him. Finally, he began to subside. Perhaps he feared he would be disciplined if he persisted. At any rate, the conference resumed in a more measured tone. No one made further reference to the accusations or sought to understand why the tirade had occurred.

Most of those present viewed this event simply as a manifestation of inappropriate behavior by an individual who was known to be given to intemperate outbursts. They were unable to see that the NA was indeed furnishing crucial information about the psychological status of the milieu. His outrage stemmed from a perception that co-workers seemed unconcerned about injuries to nurses and only wished to protect themselves. He knew that threats and injuries to nurses were treated as almost routine. Special case conferences were not convened and distinguished consultants were not invited when nurses were threatened or injured. Why then should they be concerned with the trials and tribulations of non-nurses?

The NA believed that he and his fellow nurses were regarded as cannon fodder by the hospital administration and by co-workers in other professions. Whatever degree of exaggeration and distortion one might find in his tirade, it reflected a core of accurate observation and clearly conveyed crucial information about disintegrative tensions among the staff. To some extent, it was the core of accuracy in his presentation that made it difficult for co-workers to understand and respond. A less defensive attentiveness to his material might have added new perspective to the questions surrounding the injured therapist and his violent patient.

Injuries occur on psychiatric wards for many reasons, but one crucial factor is splitting within the team. Devalued nurses tend to become resentful and to withdraw from full participation in team processes. Their presence becomes perfunctory and uncommunicative, depriving the team of vital information necessary for the maintenance of a safe environment. It has also been my observation that devalued resentful nurses tend to be less willing to risk their safety to protect co-workers.

The most effective protection against violent acting out in the milieu is a team structure that can receive, contain, and work over primitive transferences and countertransferences. This process requires open communication and trust among team members. The belief that nurses will not notice or react to attitudes of perceived indifference regarding the dangers they continually face is based on a view of nurses as devalued individuals who accept the role of victim. Hospital policies and prevailing attitudes that support or enforce this role undermine team processes and leave the milieu more chaotic and vulnerable.

IDENTIFICATION WITH THE AGGRESSOR

Devalued nurses at times treat patients in the same contemptuous and punitive manner they themselves have experienced. Or they may compensate for perceived injuries to their self-esteem by acquiring or exercising power for its own sake, sometimes at the expense of treatment considerations. Seemingly petty power struggles within the staff are typical under conditions of devaluation. They are usually described as "turf battles," but this term fails to do justice to underlying defensive needs.

The disruptive effect of power struggles can be seen when the milieu requires adjustments that impinge on functions nurses consider their private domain or in areas where they have traditionally exercised some degree of professional autonomy. Attempts to foster a relaxation of interprofessional boundaries and an integration of team functions may be felt as an assault on fragile nursing prerogatives.

Anxiety-laden preoccupation with power and boundary issues can sometimes be seen in the area of in-service education. Nurses, like other professionals in the hospital, usually have their own educational programs through which they provide training in various skills. These programs may come to represent a bastion of control and authority within a generally devaluating hospital environment.

However, certain of the most clinically crucial teaching interactions take place primarily in the interdisciplinary team meeting. Learning to receive, recognize, and contain primitive transferences is an experiential process; it requires a willingness to participate fully in case discussions, accept training from other disciplines, and to relax interpersonal and interprofessional boundaries. Clinicians who work with devalued members of the staff need to constantly remind themselves that efforts to provide educational assistance must proceed with a good deal of tact and sensitivity, since outside initiatives may be experienced as an encroachment.

Mr. G., the head nurse on one of the adult wards at Greenwood Retreat (see Chapter 2), had been prevailed upon to organize an in-service program in which members of other professional disciplines would provide a series of seminars on various topics of interest to his staff. He reluctantly appointed one of his assistants to coordinate the series but then did everything in his power to put impediments in the way, so that the seminars never took place. The assistant, who had been genuinely interested in the success of this undertaking, eventually gave up in frustration. This failure exemplifies the sort of superficial compliance accompanied by more or less hidden opposition that can occur when other professions attempt to teach without properly preparing the way.

Mr. G. was a dominating personality who left his mark on almost every aspect of the milieu. He aggressively protected nursing prerogatives, which he experienced as under unrelenting threat from other disciplines. His aggressive stance toward non-nurses enhanced the self-esteem of his staff and himself. When Mr. G. sabotaged the series of educational seminars, it was not simply another minor skirmish in a long-standing turf struggle, but represented part of a complex interpersonal and interprofessional stance that functioned to preserve a highly valued defensive equilibrium in the milieu.

After a period of soul-searching, a group of psychologists and social workers decided to invite Mr. G. to meet with them in order to discuss a limited agenda of issues having to do with achieving greater integration of team functions. Only items that were considered relatively non-controversial were included on the initial agenda.

Even the decision to invite Mr. G. was made with some trepidation. He had been known to refuse to attend similar meetings and his attitude tended to be combative and castrating. However, in this instance he rather graciously agreed to meet and interacted in a manner that seemed cordial and constructive. After about an hour, everyone had grown visibly relaxed. Some of the participants wondered why they had been so anxious and speculated that perhaps they had exaggerated Mr. G.'s hostility.

The business portion of the meeting ended on a note of cooperation but the participants lingered to chat for a while longer. With the agenda no longer present to inhibit the flow of associations, the discussion now began to stray in a number of seemingly unrelated directions, some having to do with the ward and others only peripherally connected.

Apropos of nothing in particular, Mr. G. began to talk about a group of black patients on the ward. They were, he said, feeling alone and isolated within an environment in which they were a distinct minority. He went on to empathize with these patients in a way that was highly attuned to the emotions of persons who felt endangered, outnumbered, and regarded with contempt.

Listening to these seemingly casual remarks as derivatives of Mr. G.'s unconscious transference to the group makes it possible to understand why the amicable surface feelings that prevailed during the meeting and the seemingly constructive plans for cooperation that had been formulated came to nothing. Despite the initial spirit of optimism, the psychologists and social workers soon could not help but notice an even greater degree of quiet but determined obstructionism in its day-to-day dealings with Mr. G. It gradually became apparent that none of the plans agreed upon were going to be implemented, just as the training seminars that had been agreed upon previously were never implemented.

No effort to integrate team functions on this ward could be successful without first enlisting more meaningful cooperation from Mr. G. and his staff. This formidable task would require partially diffusing the anxiety on which oppositional behavior was based. Mr. G.'s associations suggest that he was experiencing powerful feelings of devaluation, isolation, and vulnerability. Since these emotions were predominantly unconscious, they were not likely to respond to interventions based only on surface issues.

Helping co-workers build a less ambivalent and more trusting and cooperative interdisciplinary treatment effort often requires long months and years spent in working with just the sort of unconscious intrapsychic and interprofessional tensions that were present on Mr. G.'s ward. I will discuss Mr. G. and his ward again in Chapter 4, in the context of describing the role of interdisciplinary team meetings in this work.

For now, I would reiterate that seemingly petty and self-defeating turf struggles are eminently understandable in settings where devaluing status hierarchies hold sway. While realistic differences in training and experience are appropriately reflected in divisions of responsibility and authority, certain allocations of power and prestige in the psychiatric hospital have little to do with realistic functions. The persistence with which the role of nurses in the treatment milieu is misunderstood is a phenomenon that speaks to the presence of powerful irrational forces at work. My goal in this chapter has been to draw the reader's attention to the manner in which part-object tensions are entangled in this matter.

4

The Treatment Team

The focus of transference/countertransference tensions in hospital settings differs from dyadic treatment. On the ward, dynamic tensions enveloping the interdisciplinary team may constitute the most highly activated and therapeutically significant clinical development. The manner in which the team understands and responds to these tensions decisively affects the course of treatment.

Dyadic treatment is characterized by a gradually increasing focus of more or less primitive transference elements upon the person of the therapist, a process that slowly ripens in response to interpretations of activated resistances. Although he becomes the object of disturbing demands and intense feelings and fantasies, the therapist maintains a posture of technical neutrality. Departures from this norm are examined as indicative of possible countertransference influences.

In hospital treatment, the orderly unfolding of a therapeutic regression is frequently not the usual pattern. Instead, powerful and highly primitive transference reactions flare up, often expressed through actions rather than words, involving almost any member of the staff, and precipitated not by interpretations of resistance, but by certain realistic functions of the person who has become the object of the transference.

I referred to this phenomenon earlier when I noted the transferences evoked by nurses in their capacity as care-givers and limit-setters. Intense, seemingly spontaneous projections of idealized and/or persecutory part-objects appear in reaction to members of the staff whose realistic functions involve derivatives of nurturing or aggression. The physician who provides medication or signs commitment papers, the social worker who helps obtain financial benefits or arranges a foster home placement, and the psychologist who administers tests intended to probe hidden emotions may all find themselves the recipients of very disturbing primitive transferences that seem to have sprung up almost out of nowhere.

People who have chosen professions involving sublimated forms of nurturing or aggression may be highly primed to enact more primitive forms of these impulses, especially when moved to do so by projective identifications. In the course of enactment, sublimated emotions and realistic functions become linked up with precursors. In this manner, the milieu comes to function as an arena in which primitive object relations are perpetuated.

But the milieu's position at the center of transference and countertransference tensions may, under favorable circumstances, be utilized to bring into the treatment primitive transferences that might otherwise remain inaccessible, especially during relatively brief courses of therapy. Thus, milieu processes constitute both a danger and a unique opportunity. It is within this context that the therapeutic function of the team can be best understood.

RECEPTION, CONTAINMENT, WORKING
OVER, INTEGRATION

The interdisciplinary treatment team is viewed here as the milieu's organ of reception, containment, working over, and integration of part-object projections. Its task is to intercept and modify reflexive cycles of projection, enactment, and reintrojection. Team members can provide empathic understanding and the capacity to maturely cope with evoked tensions as alternatives to living out primitive object relations.

The fact that the team consists of individuals from all professional disciplines means that observations and emotional reactions funnel in from a variety of sources, situations, and perspectives. By its very constitution, the team contains the potential for both splitting and integration. Indeed, it can be thought of as an instrument for discerning and amplifying splits along factional or interpersonal fault lines.

Regarding the team as an organ of reception refers to the funneling process. Reception depends on the team having reached a level of development in which individual members experience team meetings as a safe haven where they can spontaneously report clinical material without fear of being attacked or punished. It assumes that at least some partial relaxation of intrapsychic and institutional prohibitions against experiencing and reporting anxiety-laden clinical material has been achieved.

Many teams fail to develop the capacity to funnel highly charged derivatives into meetings. I have frequently overheard informal conversations in which staff members described in vivid detail extremely significant interactions with patients. However, when these same individuals attended team meetings their contributions were sterile and empty. Not only did they not feel comfortable enough to talk freely of events on the ward, but they had little idea that their personal reactions had clinical relevance. Later in this section, I will describe working with team members to help them better observe, recognize, and report important clinical material.

The concept of containment, used here to describe a central function of the team, has been borrowed and adapted from Bion (1967). It refers to an aspect of projective identification in which a split-off component of the patient's internal world is evoked within one or more team members, often persons with a special receptivity. Containment occurs when the team member holds the identification in the psychological realm, rather than reflexively discharging it in behavior. This restraint grows out of an enhancement of conscious and unconscious observing ego functions and a heightened capacity to tolerate anxiety. In some cases, it may also involve a conscious recognition of the projection's origin in the patient.

The distinction between containment and enactment is crucial. In the well-functioning team, members funnel in experiences and observations from the milieu. The material may allude to highly charged interactions, sometimes directly involving the team member but often in derivative form (metaphors, displacements, etc.). The extent to which a member is able to bring significant material for processing is an important measure of that individual's current capacity for containment.

A crucial function of the team and of the team leader is to help members enlarge upon this capacity, to recognize or at least tolerate anxiety and other manifestations of part-object identifications, and to withstand pressure to behaviorally discharge tensions. On this level, the team is helpful simply because it encourages verbal expression of evoked derivatives, setting up an alternative space in which they may be experienced psychologically.

Processing—or working over—highly charged material has both cognitive and emotional dimensions. It is similar to Bion's concept of "detoxification," in which the more primitive and destructive qualities of projective identifications are altered through cognition and insight. In the team context, primitive derivatives are discussed, elaborated, and gradually brought under increasingly secure ego control.

An important function of the team leader in the process of working over is to help reduce anxieties, so as to enable significant material to come more fully into discussion. The leader's work is accomplished primarily through the medium of the derivative material, rather than through interpretation. This process will be discussed in greater detail later in this section.

Finally, the team functions to integrate the sometimes overwhelming and confusing clinical material—including intense emotional reactions associated with splitting—that have been funneled in from a variety of sources. Integration may involve conceptualizing or reconstructing how splits among members were evoked. In addition, the team may formulate interventions that help patients integrate dissociated experiences in the milieu.

It should be emphasized that cognitive formulations are made possible by processes of emotional integration that occur on a fairly deep level of psychological organization. The results of this in-depth work can be seen when individual team members or split-off factions are able to establish a more optimal distance from identifications with projected part-objects. During the early phases of the team's development, it is the team leader who most often facilitates this process, but as the team matures, other members more actively share the task.

DEVELOPMENT OF TEAM PROCESSES

In its initial stages, the team is not capable of reliably receiving, containing, working over, and integrating primitive projections. Before these processes can occur, it must undergo a course of development in which ground rules are securely established and mistrust diminished. Even when the team has reached a stage of effective clinical functioning, potentially disruptive anxieties and disintegrative tensions may undo much of what has been accomplished. The work done during initial stages to establish clinical functioning continues to be important later on in sustaining those functions.

During the initial stages, a primary task of the leader is to help build confidence in the team's capacity to provide safety and confidentiality. These qualities are crucial because much of the clinical material will stem from countertransference-based interactions having significant components of anxiety, aggression, sexuality, or omnipotence. These interactions often involve errors of judgment or conduct and associated feelings of guilt and embarrassment. Members will not bring highly charged material to meetings in which a punitive attitude prevails. As was suggested in Chapter 3, clinicians who wish to establish a constructive rapport with their staff have no choice but to take a long-term educational approach.

Building trust proceeds by stages and continues throughout the life of the team. In the earliest stages, it may be quite difficult to assess the most significant sources of mistrust because members participate in a guarded manner and associative processes are constricted. But with patience, good will, and the maintenance of a protected environment, the material may gradually become richer, laden with unconscious derivatives illuminating important clinical processes.

Another key factor in the process of relaxation is the clinician's respect for the legitimacy of anxieties activated in the course of daily work with very regressed and sometimes dangerous patients. Teaching efforts should proceed very slowly. Premature exploration of highly threatening areas of treatment will almost always be counterproductive.

In particular, the leader must be sensitive to the staff's fear of losing control of the milieu, a fear that can become highly inflamed by overly active efforts to foster symptom tolerance or other expressive aspects of treatment. Nursing staff has perhaps the greatest vested interest in maintaining control on the ward, since nurses and aides are most likely to suffer the consequences when it is lost. But the fear of loss of control is not by any means limited to nursing staff.

Resistance to an expressive milieu is one of many resistances that will be encountered during the course of team meetings. Often, these will have realistic as well as countertransferential origins. Efforts to mandate them out of existence or to deal with them purely on a didactic level intensify anxiety and inhibit the development of necessary processes. During the team's initial stages, the clinician can be most effective by listening carefully and respectfully, asking the right questions, and avoiding a too active stance.

RELAXATION OF ASSOCIATIONS

Within the security of a protected and respectful working environment, associational processes tend to become relatively relaxed, permitting charged derivatives of transference/countertransference tensions to make their way into the team's discussions. It is at this level that significant work in helping members disengage from identifications with projected part-objects can begin to be accomplished.

Many disintegrative tendencies in the milieu are funneled into and amplified by the team. When conditions permit, these tendencies will be expressed in indirect but comprehensible verbal material. For example, in Chapter 3, a meeting was described in which a head nurse expressed—by way of metaphor—feelings of isolation, vulnerability, and mistrust of teammates. These feelings were discharged behaviorally in a destructive turf struggle between factions of the staff. Patients were attuned to the conflict and some used it to perpetuate internal splitting.

The importance of relaxed associational processes cannot be overemphasized. I am not suggesting that team members can or should be encouraged to free associate. Well-functioning team meetings are characterized by relatively free access to clinical material that carries derivatives of transference and countertransference tensions, usually in the form of displacements, projections, or metaphor. Working with these derivatives demands therapeutic skills, but there are clear distinctions between therapy and team processes that must be respected if the leader hopes to retain the cooperation of staff. These distinctions will be described in greater detail later in this section.

Working with transference/countertransference derivatives may be disrupted by pressures to hold highly structured meetings. Staff or administrators may push for goal-oriented meetings or an otherwise structured agenda. When this initiative comes from the staff, it is frequently a sign of heightened anxiety precipitated by the potential emergence of highly charged derivatives.

For example, one frequently hears requests to devote meetings to recitations of psychological, psychiatric, and social history workups. This material is potentially useful and informative, but the format lends itself to ritualized discussions in which defensive elements dominate. Attempts to use authority or rational argument to deal with demands for greater structure are generally not very persuasive. Instead, it is necessary to identify and work with the activated anxieties that may be contributing to these demands.

There may also be pressure on the team to alter its method of conducting meetings to accommodate certain administrative requirements. Many of these are predominantly bureaucratic in nature, often involving an excessive focus on documentation or other activities that lend themselves to defensive distancing from highly charged clinical tensions. Team processes degenerate when meetings are devoted to servicing forms and documents. Under these conditions, it is difficult to cultivate the conditions that permit useful derivatives to emerge.

A too-structured agenda, whether imposed from within or without, is almost invariably used in the service of countertransference defense. I have found that an optimal degree of structure is provided when meetings are open to all observations or circumstances brought from the ward and when team members are asked to be responsible for taking the lead in choosing topics. This encourages the inclusion of a wide range of manifest content and also provides a kind of baseline against which to measure the team's functioning. Pressures to deviate from the baseline can usually be understood as indicative of the presence of activated transference/countertransference tensions.

WORKING WITHIN THE DERIVATIVE
MATERIAL

As noted above, the process of working within the derivative clinical material grows or diminishes in accordance with the vicissitudes of trust and anxiety among team members. During optimal periods, transference and countertransference tensions will be funneled into meetings. Certain elements may become apparent as team members describe their own interactions with patients. In many cases, however, significant clinical content is buried in displacements, projections, or other forms of distancing. In psychotherapy, these manifest expressions would ultimately be translated into their latent content via interpretations. In contrast, the work of the team consists of allaying and eventually containing activated tensions through elaboration of the derivative material.

The process can be seen relatively clearly in the case of a highly manipulative manic-depressive woman, Ms. T. During her many hospitalizations, Ms. T. sadistically demeaned the ward staff and was uncannily skillful in discerning their narcissistic vulnerabilities. For example, after she noticed that a certain nurse was sensitive about her weight, she never failed to make cruel and embarrassing comments regarding her appearance, often in an infuriatingly cloying tone.

As a result of this and similar behavior, Ms. T. had succeeded in getting herself wholeheartedly despised. In contrast, she talked baby-talk and behaved in a kittenish and coquettish manner with her therapist, Dr. A., who tended, against his better judgment, to overly enjoy his sessions with her and to empathize with her in her constant battles with the nursing staff.

The angry feelings harbored by nurses against Ms. T. tended to be enacted through superego mechanisms. The patient provoked this veiled sadism; her behavior was such that it was easy to believe she was being punished for her own good. Although the desire for vengeance she inspired was almost palpable, it was remarkably removed from the staff's conscious awareness.

These tensions eventually were brought into team meetings in the form of derivative material that was sufficiently clear to permit a partial working over of certain aspects of the countertransference. As a result, nurses and therapist were able to establish a more optimal distance from identifications with the patient's projected part-objects.

The clinical material involved accounts of two apparently unrelated sets of circumstances, expressed during the course of team meetings with unmistakably intense personal feeling. On the one hand, nurses described how Ms. T. evoked resentment in certain patients and gave many examples richly illustrating how she brought hatred down on herself. The second set of circumstances had to do with problems nurses were experiencing with a departmental supervisor, who was described as mistreating and abusing staff members, failing to recognize the strain they were under, and siding with others against them.

Dr. A., who was also the team leader, found himself increasingly uncomfortable as he listened to this content, especially the part having to do with the unempathic supervisor. He had always felt more than a little ashamed of the secret amusement he derived from Ms. T.'s antics on the ward and now he was hearing, in the staff's metaphor, the deep sense of injury that his identification with her sadism was causing.

Experiencing the staff's pain during team meetings helped the therapist strengthen observing ego functions, to step back from a long-standing enactment and examine his reactions more closely. He began to listen to the content of meetings more attentively than before. In thinking about the various elements of the staff's metaphor, he began to become aware of the pleasure he derived from basking in Ms. T.'s idealizations. He also suspected that he had been unconsciously supporting her attacks on the staff's self-esteem to deflect the negative transference away from himself.

As a result of his own partial disengagement from projective identifications, Dr. A. became able to work more effectively with his teammates. During subsequent meetings, he asked team members to describe in greater detail the angry feelings patients were experiencing in reaction to Ms. T. He assumed he was strengthening the metaphor they had previously provided by inviting them to project their unacceptable feelings into it more fully. He made a point of examining in detail the processes by which Ms. T. provoked hatred in her fellow patients and noted that it was not difficult to understand their reaction to her.

After a number of meetings in which interventions of this sort were repeated, Dr. A. noted that staff members were growing substantially less anxious, more receptive, and able to partially reduce metaphorical distancing. He decided that it would now be appropriate to take the work one step further. He spoke of a patient whom he had treated years before who had evoked in him feelings of hatred very similar to the feelings Ms. T. was evoking in her fellow patients. He related how ashamed he had been of being so angry at this patient, but then acknowledged, with some humor, that even doctors are human and occasionally stray from perfection. He also noted that, in retrospect, he felt he had learned a great deal from his provocative patients, especially an appreciation of how they seemed to intuit one's most sensitive areas and used that information to further their own needs.

The case of Ms. T. illustrates several aspects of working within the metaphor. First, it is apparent that someone must be able to recognize the latent content contained within the team's projections and displacements if productive work is to occur. If the leader is experiencing countertransference difficulties, he will be less likely to hear and appropriately respond. In the present example, the leader had defensively identified with an attacking and devaluing component of his patient's internalized object world and had for many weeks been oblivious to material that might have disturbed the equilibrium he had achieved.

At least two factors contributed to a shift in this equilibrium. First, Dr. A. had from the beginning experienced some degree of unease with his partially conscious identification with Ms. T.'s acting out. The countertransference enactment had never become entirely ego-syntonic; he was struggling with it internally quite apart from what was transpiring in the team. The increasingly clear derivative material aided the process of disengagement.

The second factor, which worked in tandem with the first, involved the team's internal cohesion and capacity to funnel in productive derivatives even though intense countertransference tensions were operative. This capacity grew out of the team's long history of work together, during which an atmosphere of mutual respect and confidence had evolved. Although team members were hurt by the leader's seeming to side with the patient against them, they were able to bring this feeling to meetings in verbal form, rather than attacking or disrupting the team. This capacity to sustain work under stress is similar in many respects to the therapeutic alliance.

For Ms. T., attacking and devaluing care-givers expressed partially conscious rage at a psychotic mother who had, she felt, allowed her to be repeatedly injured as a child and who had exploited and betrayed her as an adult. In her relations with Dr. A., the rage was conspicuously absent. Treatment involved an unconscious collusion that permitted the patient and Dr. A. to bask in an experience of mutual admiration and omnipotent protective care. Only after he had sufficiently recovered from his own difficulties could Dr. A. help team members disengage from their participation in Ms. T.'s primitive object relations.

The first task was to recognize and accept the operative metaphor. The staff was clearly attempting to persuade itself that only patients hated Ms. T. Staff members could not experience their own hatred because doing so violated personal and professional ideals and prohibitions. Their predominant defense was enactment. Ms. T.'s highly dramatized infractions were punished in a manner that permitted discharge of vengeful sadistic impulses, but they also provided a rationale that kept these feelings out of awareness.

The goal in working with the metaphor was to use it as a vehicle for allaying the staff's guilt and anxiety. By working over the minute details of the anger in its projected form, staff members gradually grew less threatened. The increased mastery that can be fostered in this manner can be quite impressive. At times, anxiety is reduced to the point that even the metaphor itself can be relinquished by some members of the team.

More frequently, work within the metaphor permits staff to make trial or tentative contact with unconscious impulses and anxiety. Displacement and projection are maintained but the degree of distancing is reduced and defensive structures become less rigid. Work within the metaphor reduces the need to resort to more regressive and destructive modes of defense, such as acting out.

Dr. A. asked team members to explain in detail how Ms. T. was able to elicit such passionate hatred in her fellow patients. By focusing on her provocations, he hoped to convey that intense negative reactions to her were an understandable human response and not necessarily a sign of depravity. He acknowledged that he could well understand why certain patients were so angry. He was careful, however, to emphasize a distinction between feelings and vindictive actions.

Finally, Dr. A. departed from the metaphor provided by the staff and offered one of his own. He proceeded in this fashion because the previous work had gone well and he believed team members were ready to work with material that was a few steps closer to underlying anxieties. By shifting the discussion from the anger of patients to his own anger at a provocative patient, he was implicitly asking staff to tolerate the idea that not only patients experience forbidden affects and fantasies. Yet he was also respecting the defensive distancing that was still needed.

Dr. A. emphasized his struggle with shame and guilt and his failure to live up to perfectionistic standards. He avoided excessive self-disclosure but provided enough information to implicitly invite staff members to identify with the emotional storm he had more or less successfully weathered. His use of self-deprecating humor was intended to deflate the grandiosity implicit in the belief that anyone could remain untouched by inner doubts and dystonic emotions in the course of work with patients such as Ms. T.

COGNITIVE LEARNING IN THE TEAM

Team processes can foster a climate of psychological safety in which cognitive learning more effectively takes place. Certain of Dr. A.'s interventions noted above were partially didactic. For example, demonstrating how anger is provoked, describing anger as an inevitable human reaction, and suggesting that such reactions are a potential source of useful information were all interventions that had a teaching dimension.

In a sense, Dr. A.'s topic was the continuity of human experience. The team's projection of its hatred of Ms. T. onto patients was based in part on the assumption that certain emotions and fantasies are sick and only to be found in sick persons. Externalizations of this sort are often supported by misinformation, such as the notion that mentally ill and healthy persons function in entirely different ways.

Dr. A. acknowledged that he could empathize with the

hatred patients experienced toward Ms. T. because he had, in fact, struggled with such hatred himself. By making this information available, he encouraged trial identifications with externalized emotions and fantasy.

The usual problem with teaching on the wards is that anxiety-inducing information is defensively warded off. If it is to be usefully absorbed, the level of anxiety must be diminished. Under favorable conditions, team members can use accurate information about the workings of interpersonal and intrapersonal processes to augment their ability to contain evocations of primitive object relations. Since many will not have had personal psychotherapeutic experiences, the cognitive learning that takes place in team meetings assumes a heightened relative significance.

INDIRECT INTERPRETATIONS

Working within the metaphor supports a higher level equilibrium of transference/countertransference tensions. It should be kept in mind that team members cannot be expected to directly confront their unconscious processes. It is important that the leader respect the limits within which teammates are willing and able to work. Teams can often deal with dystonic material at a closer but still safe distance. Determining an optimal degree of safety requires a good deal of clinical sensitivity. The leader uses the metaphor to bring the underlying latent content and its associated anxiety closer to consciousness. But if this process is handled clumsily or if it proceeds too far or too quickly, it will be experienced as invasive and will arouse an unworkable level of anxiety, mistrust, and anger.

Interpretation of unconscious processes in team members is almost always a serious error. Dr. A. understood but did not interpret the hatred felt by his co-workers. Instead, he focused on the efforts patients were making to be polite to Ms. T. His suggestion that they were probably feeling ashamed of their hatred was an indirect interpretation, intended to bring the dynamic relationship between hatred, shame, and "politeness" closer to awareness without overly challenging necessary projections.

Indirect interpretations may also involve identifying intense affects that have become more or less transformed via euphemistic descriptions of clinical material. For example, Dr. A. pointed out that patients were much more than simply upset with Ms. T.; they were feeling enraged and murderous toward her. Clarifications of this sort encourage trial identifications with projected or displaced constellations of feeling and fantasy.

REALISTIC CORRECTIVE MEASURES

It may be helpful now to briefly take note of a closely related process that occurs during work with the team. Frequently, the derivative material brought into team meetings illuminates structural fault lines or other realistic features of the milieu that support part-object projections. Working over the derivatives of these splits may be ineffectual if the realistic component has reached a certain magnitude of importance. In these circumstances, it may sometimes be possible to make use of the insights garnered by the team to make appropriate modifications in the dysfunctional structure.

The complexities and frustrations inherent in attempts to work with structuralized splits can be illustrated by returning to an earlier example in which a head nurse, Mr. G., expressed via projection and metaphor unconscious feeling of being outnumbered and devalued by teammates.

Mr. G. was a formidable person who seemed always primed to lash out with sarcastic and demeaning comments. By example and precept, he encouraged his staff to relate to psychiatric patients as transgressors and to rely on punishment and devaluation to deal with the more refractory ones. Psychologists and social workers tended to react with an overly protective stance. This split had become structuralized in various procedures, attitudes, rivalries, and alliances. It was frequently exacerbated by patients who used it to live out a variety of primitive fantasies.

Mr. G.'s sense of narcissistic vulnerability and of being under attack was long-standing and unlikely to be significantly reduced by team processes. But it was continually being unnecessarily exacerbated, with a resulting intensification of enactments in which Mr. G. made use of ward circumstances to do battle against those whom he perceived as attempting to belittle and defeat him.

For example, the staff meeting in which Mr. G. metaphorically expressed feeling under attack (see Chapter 3) was called without consulting him. Psychologists and social workers wanted to discuss certain ward functions that Mr. G. was known to regard as falling within his personal domain. He was informed of the impending meeting by a delegation of team members who asked him to be present. Not only was he in fact outnumbered, but he accurately suspected that the meeting's unspoken agenda involved criticism of him and his department.

The form of the invitation confirmed Mr. G.'s suspicion that he was regarded as a likely adversary. The fact that a special invitation was needed for a person who played such a key role in the milieu was a sign of serious dysfunction. The meeting brought into sharper focus the fact that Mr. G. had not been willing to participate as a regular member of the team and that his absence had become part of the milieu's customary manner of operating.

The associations that emerged in the meeting illuminated an underlying meaning of Mr. G.'s aggressive adversarial stance that had not been previously discernible. The ward's chronic structural split was tied to specific personal anxieties. Mr. G.'s hostile castrating persona and the procedures and alliances that grew out of it were to some extent defensive in nature. The ward organization, with its nursing staff girded to do battle with psychologists and social workers, expressed his experience of imminent threat and externalized his fight for self-esteem.

Having a clearer picture of Mr. G.'s vulnerability would not bring change to a long-standing personal equilibrium. But if the derivatives that emerged within the team meeting were recognized and treated with the seriousness they deserved, staff members would be in a much better position to make realistic adjustments in their approach to Mr. G., taking into consideration his anxieties and defensive style. Thus, it might become possible to move in the direction of more integrated participation or at least toward a less confrontational stance.

In summary, highly charged derivatives that emerge in team meetings may make it possible to assess and locate the source(s) of disintegrative tensions. There are two closely related ways to work with splits. First, when a structural dimension has been identified, its impact may be diminished via corrective interventions or realistic adjustments. Second, splits projected into the team by patients are contained, worked over, and integrated on a derivative level. Realistic corrective actions and the working over process are frequently intertwined, since projective identifications often involve persons and groups with preexisting (structuralized) tendencies to split.

FACTORS THAT SUPPORT OR BLOCK TEAM PROCESSES

I noted earlier that the treatment team is more likely to develop the capacity to contain and work over primitive emotional tensions under favorable conditions of work, but I did not identify those conditions. In the material to follow, I will describe certain characteristics of settings where effective clinical teams developed, characteristics that were absent or considerably altered in less successful settings.

Clinical teams that are able to consistently and systematically funnel in, contain, and elaborate transference/countertransference derivatives appear to be fairly rare, but those that serve only defensive and discharge needs are probably even more rare. Of the many hospitals discussed in these pages, Midtown Psychiatric Center seemed most able to provide the predisposing factors that favored effective team processes, but even at MPC such teams were the exception. Thus, it may be instructive to compare successful and unsuccessful wards at MPC and also to examine ways in which MPC differed from other settings.

First, MPC was a teaching hospital and had traditionally involved its personnel in a range of training and other support activities. When I first joined the staff, I had just completed a two-year internship during which I had worked mostly with relatively intact outpatients. Coming onto the ward was a jarring and disorienting experience and it took me several months to settle down to some degree. During that period, my level of anxiety was such that I was constantly moving in the direction of taking on dysfunctional but comforting ways of coping and relating. Fortunately, my clinical supervisor was an experienced and skillful person who saw that I needed a good deal of assistance and was willing to provide it. In addition to steadying me, he introduced me to the notion of the milieu as a functioning dynamic entity and to the use of team processes to gain access to its unconscious tensions.

A few years later, on a different ward, I had the good fortune to work with a consultant whose understanding of the inner world of regressed patients illuminated aspects of primitive mental functioning that had seemed all but incomprehensible. My interest and enthusiasm for my work was rekindled by this experience. Looking back, I can see how the grinding tensions and confusions of years on the wards had depleted me and how my efforts were taking on a perfunctory and emotionally distanced quality. Clearly, I had sorely needed a better grasp of my discipline's possibilities in order to work more creatively.

Much of what I have written here involves an attempt to integrate and further develop what I learned from these two gifted clinicians. My exposure to teachers of this caliber was not unique at MPC. The hospital provided its staff with a rich learning environment. Each of the mental health disciplines maintained active training programs. A full schedule of seminars, case conferences, and clinical supervision were offered by senior hospital clinicians and consultants from the local psychoanalytic institute. Staff members as well as students participated in many of these activities. Ongoing educational processes provided much needed emotional support, as well as serving as a source of new information and skills.

At MPC, it was unusual to encounter co-workers who had not had some contact with notions of internal motivation and levels of psychological functioning. Although many understood mental and emotional dysfunction primarily in terms of biochemical processes, few were unaware of alternative modes of conceptualization and practice. Thus, it was often possible to evoke at least some reluctant or ambivalent interest in psychodynamic processes, even on wards where chemical management was the treatment modality of choice.

In contrast, exposure to psychological concepts and methods was more limited at the other settings discussed here. The disparity was very apparent and telling in its consequences, especially among members of the nursing staff. Efforts to enlist the cooperation of nurses in milieu treatment were likely to be experienced as incomprehensible and to meet with suspicion or active opposition at many of these settings. In general, there was less receptivity to psychological thinking and less workable ambivalence. The staff tended, on the whole, to be more defensive and parochial in outlook. Clearly, MPC's policy of including ward staff in clinical education activities had produced significant results.

In attempting to understand my contrasting experiences with teams and settings, I have found the idea of a "critical mass" to be useful. On wards where an effective milieu developed, there was always a small but significant core of potentially receptive staff. This core, or consensus, had sometimes taken considerable time and effort to evolve, but it was present in every case. On wards where the influence of the core group had failed to reach a critical threshold, little or no headway was made in using team processes to assess and reduce countertransference enactment.

The existence of sophisticated training programs and the probability of having at least a few like-minded colleagues helped make MPC more open to the development of team processes. However, these conditions were not in themselves sufficient. Most wards at MPC never developed effective teams. Both at MPC and elsewhere, there appeared to be other variables that entered into the equation in a decisive fashion.

One such factor involved the presence or absence of a stable dynamic equilibrium or defensive balance in the milieu. Where such a balance was absent or tenuous, anxiety, upheaval, and tensions were close to the surface. In such circumstances, offering a way to understand and contain tensions might meet with a receptive welcome.

In contrast, wards where a stable equilibrium had been achieved were characterized by relatively unworkable resistances, often sustained by projective identification, enactment, emotional disengagement, and institutionally sanctioned countertransference structures. On these wards, a serious psychodynamic interest in the milieu was likely to be experienced as disruptive and threatening.

I worked in relative isolation on a number of such wards and never succeeded in establishing a strong relationship with the staff. Most typically, I felt myself regarded as an outsider, a threat to an established order. My feeling of frustration and failure was especially painful because I had had very gratifying experiences in working with teams and had come to consider myself something of an expert. But these wards forced me to acknowledge that I had overestimated my capacities and underestimated the importance of working in a relatively supportive environment.

Unfortunately, effective treatment teams are fragile; they take time, effort, and patience to build up and are susceptible to a variety of potentially disruptive clinical and off-ward influences. When I left MPC, working with teams had become more difficult than ever. The hospital was increasingly being forced to comply with mandates from a seemingly endless list of regulatory and accrediting bodies, many of which were naive and time-consuming at best, and irrational and destructive at worst. One result was that clinical activities and interpersonal relationships within the team were increasingly distorted by bureaucratic methods and priorities.

I will describe this process in more detail in Chapter 6. For now, I will only note that the intrusion of bureaucratic functions severely undermined team meetings as a clinical process at MPC. Meetings became ritualized, obsessive, and devoted to servicing documents, remote from the highly charged aliveness of the ward. As discussions grew more constricted, access to primitive unconscious processes diminished and defensive barriers between and within team members rigidified. With the growing incapacitation of the team, there seemed to be much less to be done to allay the effects of countertransference enactment in the milieu.

5

The Therapeutic Alliance

THE THERAPIST AS AGENT

The therapist is considered a helping person, but whom or what do we help? A number of competing interests and values lay claim to our loyalty. Patients, especially those who see us in private practice and who pay fees, expect us to work on their behalf. They regard us as their agent, but each defines his expectations very differently, sometimes in ways we cannot endorse. For example, we frequently encounter prospective patients who in essence want us to induce other persons to treat them differently. In such circumstances, we usually do not agree to serve as the patient's advocate. Instead we regard the assumption that he plays no role in creating and sustaining his difficulties as a focus of concern.

This example suggests that therapists do not function simply as agents of their patients' demands but are also guided by certain rules of craftsmanship and assumptions about the workings of the personality. The two sets of loyalties exist in a sort of shifting balance. Potentially disruptive conflicts between the patient's wishes and the needs of treatment occur during intensifications of the transference but are often responsive to interpretations, thus permitting the patient to gain insight and to return to an acceptance of the basic ground rules (Langs 1973). Therapists are generally more comfortable with patients who can make this shift because underlying conflicts between the patient's desires and those of the therapist are kept within relatively tolerable limits.

With more disturbed patients, however, it is often the case that such conflicts are far less readily resolved. Instead, therapists are frequently exposed to the disturbing sensation of being at odds with the person they are supposed to be helping. This engenders a great deal of confusion and distress. Some therapists attempt to resolve it by identifying with one or another side of the conflict.

In many treatment settings, a more or less adversarial treatment relationship is considered unavoidable. Certain diagnoses are thought to mandate that the therapist function as an agent of mental health norms and external reality. Opposing the illness entails opposing the person who has the illness if, against all rhyme and reason, he refuses to accept the therapist's helpful guidance.

At the settings surveyed here, most therapists tended to dismiss the often bizarre demands of their severely disturbed patients as artifacts of a disease process, rather than as expressions of human experience worthy of serious consideration. Many therapists were troubled by the conflict-ridden relationships this stance engendered. Yet they could conceive of no other way to help.

Hospital therapists must also contend with a variety of confusing demands and expectations emanating from outside the therapeutic dyad. Frequently, they are called upon to act at the behest of alarmed or concerned or angry family members. Social service agencies and law enforcement officials also expect cooperation. Perhaps most crucially, therapists are subjected to immense pressures from within the ward and the hospital. The more disturbed, violent, or disruptive a patient's behavior, the more insistent and pervasive are the external demands intruding into the therapy.

The presence of powerful external demands raises again the question of whom the therapist helps. The dilemma is further clouded because external demands are frequently viewed as essentially indistinguishable from mental health norms. Most therapists who act as agents for various parties outside the dyad seem to regard their actions as a necessary extension of the effort to enhance mental health.

For example, I have known cases in which hospital therapists and social workers assisted in having patients unwillingly removed from their homes at the request of family members who felt that the responsibility of care had grown too burdensome. How was it that mental health professionals considered it their duty to facilitate these evictions? Each person in these wrenching family tragedies had legitimate needs at stake. Were staff members acting unwittingly as agents of social control? Were they victims of role confusion? Or perhaps they had not considered that families could turn to a variety of other persons or agencies to work on their behalf.

Those who assisted in these and similar interventions were able to more or less dismiss the feelings of betrayal evoked by their actions. They strongly felt that their patients' demands could not be taken as seriously as the demands of nonpatients, that a desire to remain in the family home, for example, was unrealistic or inappropriate or regressive. By pathologizing these longings, they felt obliged to oppose them, to align with family members who also opposed them, and to insist on providing "healthier" and more "realistic" living arrangements.

It is clear that many severely disturbed patients appear to give every indication of needing to be dealt with in a manner that renders the concept of a treatment alliance more or less irrelevant. The crucial importance of relating to such patients as potentially responsible collaborators is not always intuitively obvious. In addition, it requires a quality of emotional engagement not easily achieved or sustained.

In contrast, a unilateral approach—in which patients are acted upon at the discretion of staff—is more immediately responsive to the staff's desire to make things better, to be caring and conscientious in its duties. Much less visibly, the unilateral approach provides important channels for enactments that enhance the staff's security. The infantilizing nature of these enactments is not easily recognized because they so closely resemble the ordinary and expected forms of unilateral practice.

When applied in the heat of difficult clinical situations, the unilateral approach may have little connection to an informed view of treatment, illness, or health. Interventions and norms may be tailored to rationalize all sorts of enactments needed to ward off primitive anxiety. The definition of appropriate behavior often shifts according to the staff's current psychological equilibrium. The clinical material presented throughout this book illustrates the readiness with which unconscious needs and fears infiltrate norms, treatment ideologies, and interventions.

The question of therapist as agent is further complicated by the confusing complexity of patients' demands. For example, patients who loudly proclaim their wish to be free of restrictive rules and structures may put immense pressure on the therapist and the milieu to enact omnipotent control or punishment. Or patients who cry out for attachment and nurturing may skillfully defeat all attempts to provide assistance, evoking instead rejection and hatred.

Therapist as Agent of Social Control

Some writers have examined the demands impinging on hospital therapists and concluded that conflicts of interest are not resolvable. Szasz, for example, has described involuntary psychiatric hospitalization as an instrumentality of social control (1961). He posits an inherent contradiction between the goals and values of society and those of psychiatry. Psychiatry's ethics and identity have been compromised and disoriented by its willingness to function as an agent of society, according to Szasz.

Szasz also rejects the concept of mental illness and appears to regard psychological norms as arbitrary social conventions that suppress or distort authentic personal needs. The purpose of therapy is to assist each person in developing his or her own unique solutions to problems in living (1965). The therapist carefully refrains from promoting or imposing his own preconceptions. Szasz refers to this process as "autonomous psychotherapy."

According to the more extreme adherents of the Szaszian view, any normative concept of mental health or of psychological development—or even a general view of personality—transforms the therapist into an agent of established conventions. Within this perspective, the notion of autonomy takes on an absolute moral imperative, just as "mental health" takes on a transcendent and moralistic connotation among practitioners of normative therapy.

A PSYCHOANALYTIC PERSPECTIVE

Psychoanalytic treatment has historically been concerned with fostering psychological growth, enhancing expressivity, and diminishing anxieties that cripple the capacity to love and work. Its method involves a serious and systematic consideration of the inner perspective of persons struggling to define themselves. It is a process that cannot unfold in the absence of a collaborative alliance between therapist and patient.

The alliance is not a static or monolithic entity; its components wax and wane in response to shifts in the transference. The fact that the patient's needs, demands, and expectations cannot be acceded to is—from the analytic perspective—neither surprising nor necessarily disturbing. In fact, such conflicts constitute a central focus of the work.

Disturbances in the relationship of therapist and patient are examined in terms of their defensive, adaptive, and structural significance. The patient is treated as a responsible participant who has much to gain from understanding their meanings, origins, and implications. The therapist's commitment to the procedures of his work does not imply an agenda of values to be imposed on the patient's life outside the treatment hour. In most circumstances the ground rules can be regarded as a sort of baseline against which deviations are measured, examined, and understood.

But can the way of thinking and working described above be applied to individuals whose reality testing, impulse control, and self-observation may at times be overwhelmed or distorted to a degree that seems to rule out any semblance of an alliance? The difficulties reflected by this question can be seen in the fact that, until relatively recently, analytic therapists have, with a few significant exceptions, chosen not to work with very fragile or primitive or psychotic patients. Within the context of the present discussion, one might say that a conceptual framework and technical procedures were not available to cope with the seemingly insurmountable opposition of demands and loyalties presented by these patients.

However, with the maturation of psychoanalytic ego psychology, a framework has developed that permits a fuller and more systematic basis for understanding the impairments of severely disturbed individuals and for conducting therapy in the absence of a stable alliance. These developments have widened the scope of psychological treatment to include persons and diagnostic groups previously considered untreatable. They have also cast the question of the therapist's loyalty in a new and somewhat more productive light.

A helpful historical introduction to the extensive literature on ego psychology, especially as applied to patients with structural dysfunction, is provided by Blanck and Blanck (1974). Current clinical and theoretical approaches to primitive patients incorporating both ego psychological and object relations perspectives is available in the work of Kernberg (1976, 1980), Giovacchini and Boyer (1982), and Ogden (1982, 1989).

Ego psychological conceptions of mental illness and of the treatment process have evolved in large measure from the insights of Anna Freud. Her recommendation (1936) that the analyst assume a position equidistant from id, ego, and superego is especially germane. Early in its historical development, psychoanalysis had emphasized the task of bringing dissociated impulses into consciousness. For Anna Freud, however, "the ego is itself the object of analysis . . . very much like the unconscious activity of the prohibited instinctual impulses" (p. 30).

Anna Freud recognized that access to the libido proceeds through and depends upon modification of ego defensive structures. Self-observing functions of the ego may become aligned with and support the analytic work. At times, however, the "analyst's aim in bringing the unconscious into consciousness and the efforts of the ego to master instinctual life are contrary to one another" (p. 29). This observation clearly suggests that a central task of treatment is to strengthen those ego functions that enhance the patient's ability to participate. Thus, the therapist becomes an agent of healthier ego functioning as well as of libidinal expressivity.

Hartmann's conception of the ego's executive and adaptive functions (Hartmann 1958, 1964) is also pertinent here. By viewing the ego as an organization of executive and regulatory functions with adaptive as well as defensive dimensions, Hartmann provided a powerful conceptual tool for treating severely disturbed patients. His view of the ego as regulating psychological equilibria and mediating the demands of internal and external reality is especially important for a psychoanalytic conception of regressive symptomatology.

In the case discussions here, I emphasize viewing symptoms as attempts to master psychological tensions and to establish a more or less stable balance in the ego. For the analytic therapist, symptoms are understood as accomplishments as well as indications of pathology. According to this view, crude or coercive or premature attempts to extirpate symptoms may disrupt ego functions and lead to increased regression.

Anna Freud's concept of equidistance and Hartmann's view of the ego as comprising a complex organization of regulatory and adaptive functions can be understood as implying a stance in which the therapist may, depending on the ego's current balance, serve as an agent of regulation, of ideals and prohibitions, of defense against overwhelming anxiety, of adaptation, or of emerging drive derivatives.

From the perspective of equidistance, countertransference can be seen as the therapist's identification with one psychological agency at the expense of all others. The symptom controller, for example, may be aligned with primitive superego precursors in his patient and himself when he administers treatments that are thinly veiled forms of attack and omnipotent control. In the same vein, adherents of unlimited autonomy may unwittingly align themselves with destructive primitive urges that threaten to overwhelm tenuous ego functions.

The ego psychology perspective makes possible a relatively sophisticated approach to mental and emotional dysfunction based on psychological observation. It allows mental conditions to be understood and treated on a case-by-case basis, in terms of clinical criteria, rather than confronted as deviations from social or mental health norms.

For the ego psychologist, as for others, the question of whom the therapist works for is most perplexing with patients whose behavior is dangerous but ego-syntonic and who show little or no apparent capacity to enter into a collaborative alliance. Ego psychology does not offer an easy-to-apply formula that can be readily discerned and followed in such cases.

Its virtue is that it keeps the most significant questions open so that they may be continually rediscovered in the clinical material and renegotiated. It fosters a stance in which the therapist observes and weighs conflicting needs and shifting balances as they occur rather than adopting a rigid ideological allegiance to abstractions such as "mental health" or "autonomy." This perspective is immensely helpful with patients who defensively transform intrapsychic tensions into interpersonal conflicts that are then evoked and lived out in the milieu.

UNILATERAL TREATMENT AS COUNTERTRANSFERENCE STRUCTURE

With these introductory comments, we can now turn to the central theme of this chapter, an examination of the role of the therapeutic alliance in the transference/countertransference equilibrium. Specifically, I will be suggesting that a crucial function of the alliance is to provide orientation for therapists as they come under the sway of tensions that evoke distancing, dehumanization, and omnipotent control. Respect for the alliance helps to humanize the treatment relationship and buffers it from encroachments of the therapist's omnipotence.

The discussion will focus on a key dimension of the alliance, referred to here as the *collaborative relationship.* Collaboration is defined as two parties working together, each bringing his or her own special skill and knowledge, embarking upon a shared project, the outcome of which cannot be defined or dictated in advance by either party. The collaborative relationship is contrasted with the *unilateral* treatment relationship in which one party, in the role of expert, generates goals and performs interventions upon a second party, often a person of diminished status, who is supposed to more or less passively receive those goals and interventions.

Clearly, there are gradations of collaboration. As the case material will demonstrate, collaboration does not emerge spontaneously; it is the product of work by both parties. Frequently, there are strong barriers standing in the way of such work. Patient and therapist often experience anxieties and distortions that appear to rule out working together in a cooperative mode. The therapist's misgivings are further intensified when the patient—as often happens—engages in behavior that exerts a strong pull for unilateral measures. In these circumstances, the manifest content of a behavior or symptom may be reflexively reacted to, rather than understood as a complex evocation in which the therapist is being cast in a role originating in the patient's inner world.

Acting Out

In the settings surveyed here, unilateral methods were typically viewed as vital for controlling acting out. The attribution of acting out justified a wide range of interventions, many of them coercive and infantilizing. Because its influence on hospital treatment is so powerful, I will examine the concept in some detail.

In its original meaning, acting out refers to a resistance in which feelings and fantasies emerging in the transference are lived out in some fashion. It is viewed as resistance because it involves substitution of behavior for remembering, often takes place away from the scrutiny of the therapy process, and usually signals an attenuation of observing ego functions and weakening of the therapeutic alliance.

In many hospital settings, acting out is understood in an exclusively behavioral sense, a way of labeling conduct as sick, inappropriate, and intolerable. Often, there is little recognition that it was intended as a descriptive, not a pejorative, term. In essence, a technical concept with certain restricted meanings has come to function as an all-purpose rationale for aggression-saturated intervention.

Acting out is not a useful term without an understanding of its structural, dynamic, and transference context. A comprehensive and in-depth assessment is required to weigh the impact of potential interventions. In particular, it is crucial to understand the function of the acting out as it relates to the patient's attempts to master internal tensions. The anxieties and impulses that fuel behavior are much more difficult to recognize and understand if the behavior is viewed according to a crude dichotomy of appropriate versus inappropriate. In the absence of a psychological context, management techniques are highly susceptible to infiltration by countertransference tensions. The result is often staff acting out in response to patient acting out.

A patient hospitalized at a state facility repeatedly appeared at the nursing station and made provocative and disturbingly graphic sexual remarks and gestures. Initially, the nurses were merely annoyed, but as the provocation escalated, they became anxious and angry. They attended the next team meeting en masse and demanded that a management plan be instituted. After much discussion of possible interventions, it was decided that the patient would be placed in seclusion if he persisted.

The offending behavior continued and the patient was taken to the seclusion room according to plan. Once there, he stripped off his clothes, urinated on the floor, and pounded on the door until the late hours of the night, disrupting the entire ward. When nurses periodically came to observe him, he openly masturbated. He became increasingly agitated and disorganized; it took several days and many injections of neuroleptic medication before he calmed down somewhat.

The reaction to the patient's acting out involved two serious errors: first, staff members were unable to contain their angry reaction to the highly aggressive elements in the patient's behavior. Second, they failed to understand that his disturbed behavior involved an attempt to establish some semblance of inner equilibrium, that it was not directed solely at them. The patient's return to the nursing station day after day signaled distress and a need for soothing, admiration, and nurturing. When forcibly deprived of a comparatively compensated level of exhibitionistic defense, he shifted to a much more primitive narcissistic regression.

Once the patient's conduct had been characterized as inappropriate acting out, no further assessment was thought to be needed. The tapestry of meanings, impulses, and fears that found representation in his behavior was left unexamined. It was accepted as a matter of course that management could be accomplished only by means of aggressive measures and that the patient was incapable of working together with the staff to better contain and understand the behavior that had so dramatically thrust him into everyone's awareness.

The patient evoked hatred, disgust, and fear in the nursing staff. The management plan succeeded in discharging and warding off these feelings. However, dealing with the patient in this manner intensified the primitive anxiety that had brought him to the nursing station in the first place: the fear of becoming nonexistent to the persons who were taking care of him.

Throughout this process, the concept of acting out was repeatedly cited to disguise and justify aggressive measures. The exclusive focus on actions distanced the staff from connectedness with the individual who acted, just as his actions distanced him from intolerable feelings. Distancing facilitated a relatively guilt-free attack. The result, as noted, was a severe iatrogenic regression.

Misapplication of the concept of acting out reflects more than lack of understanding of a familiar clinical term. On the wards, the distortion functions as a highly effective countertransference structure, justifying and disguising countertherapeutic enactments. A close conceptual cousin, "inappropriate behavior," is frequently misused in the same fashion.

Working effectively with primitive anxieties and drive

derivatives requires a multi-layered approach to disturbing behavior. For example, ostensibly sexual behavior—as in the case above—may involve a variety of functions, not all of which have genitality as a primary focus. Pregenital and genital strivings and compensatory processes are not infrequently lumped together under the rubric of "sexual acting out." Management measures should include an understanding of the behavior's structural, dynamic, and transference/countertransference context.

Certain sexual constellations appear very frequently and should be easily recognized. Examples that come to mind are the heterosexual seductiveness of impending homosexual panic and the promiscuity that wards off depression, worthlessness, and fear of abandonment. In both cases, the manifest sexual behavior protects against an overwhelming loss of equilibrium and may be crucial in preventing further decompensation.

A clinical approach to patients threatened with massive regression involves carefully balancing the requirements of a safe and orderly milieu with an appreciation for the disintegrative impact of primitive anxiety. Cautious interpretations directed toward areas of ego dysfunction are combined with a firm but tactful rechanneling of the most disruptive aspects of the overt sexuality.

Limit setting is often an important component of this process, but limits are better tolerated if negotiated in a collaborative and respectful spirit. Aggressive unilateral measures cannot always be avoided, but in too many cases their use reflects a failure to foster cooperation and a need for enactment channels. In the settings examined here, enactments of omnipotent control were invariably a greater danger to the treatment process than was a paucity of controls.

The treatment team may at times have great difficulty in distinguishing between appropriate management and disguised enactment. Disturbances not infrequently arise that require the assistance of a consultant who is not caught up in the day to day tensions of the milieu. Any sustained diminution in the team's capacity to foster collaboration with its patients should be regarded as a possible signal indicating a need for consultation.

Alienation and Self-Loathing

As we have seen, disturbed behavior may evoke and be perpetuated by the ward staff's retreat from collaborative working relationships. The staff will be especially likely to retreat in response to behavior that is experienced as repellent. Such behavior plays a key role in the dynamics of the milieu; thus it is important to understand that it tends to develop out of a characteristic psychological context. In this section, the focus will be on the primitive patient's self-loathing and sense of malignant destructiveness, and on the processes through which this disturbed sense of self evokes revulsion, hatred, punishment, and distancing that infiltrate treatment efforts and increase reliance on aggression-saturated unilateral measures.

The inner world of primitive patients is dominated by forms of relatedness in which omnipotence, murderous rage, and fear of annihilation prevail, and in which loving attachments are experienced as inherently devouring and destructive. Unconsciously—and sometimes consciously—these individuals experience themselves as irredeemable, insatiable, and inhuman, akin to monsters or criminals. In projecting aggression-saturated part-objects into the interpersonal world, they attempt to rid themselves of danger. But the vengefulness and revulsion they elicit instead tends to validate and intensify their paranoid fears.

The offer of therapeutic assistance is especially threatening because it exacerbates ineffable regressive longings for nurturance and symbiotic merger. Out of envy, hatred, and fear, the patient is powerfully motivated to alienate and defeat potential helpers. In so doing, he creates a more desperate experience of isolation and futility. He may also succeed in realistically transforming the potential helper.

Perhaps I can bring the evocation of loathing into sharper focus by recounting a clinical interaction in which I was overcome by an experience of almost unbearable hatred and repulsion. At the time, it felt as though my consciousness had been invaded by shameful and alien emotions that I could not shut out or dispel. Although I did not handle this situation well, it contributed to my education in an unforgettable manner, demonstrating with undeniable power the uncanny ability of primitive patients to induce identifications with their inner experience.

The patient in question, Mr. C., was a newly admitted middle-aged man who had achieved a high level of functioning prior to the onset of his illness. The illness itself was ambiguous. Several previous therapists had concluded that Mr. C. suffered irreversible brain damage when he swallowed a large number of pills in a suicide attempt a few years earlier. Others thought he was chronically schizophrenic.

One reason for the uncertainty was that the patient was extremely withdrawn and uncommunicative. His slovenly appearance, apathy, and unfriendliness discouraged attempts to know him better. I noted, in this regard, a barely disguised relief among staff members when he rebuffed attempts to draw him into conversation. He exuded a foul odor, apparently the result of refusing to wash himself. After a week of futile efforts to keep him bathed and in clean clothing, the nursing staff had given up and left Mr. C. pretty much to his own devices.

As I recall, I first approached the patient in a rather sympathetic and confident manner. I had been struck by the tragic disparity between his previous life and the condition in which I now found him. I did not regard him as hopeless. To the contrary, I thought the pessimism of his previous therapists was premature. It seemed likely I could do better.

It soon became apparent, however, that the patient was not welcoming my efforts. Although he silently followed me to the interview room, his attitude very powerfully conveyed a desire to be left alone. As we sat together, he slowly but discernibly shifted his attention away from me and from anything I attempted to say to him. After about 15 minutes, I could see that my efforts to establish contact were having an opposite effect; he was gradually becoming increasingly oblivious to my presence.

At first, I was not greatly concerned. I was accustomed to withdrawn patients. There was no need to rush matters; I would sit patiently with Mr. C. and he would eventually come around a bit.

I now noticed that the patient had inserted an index finger into his nasal cavity and was exploring the contents with an air of fixed attention. At first, this behavior had not impressed me as particularly remarkable. But I soon became struck by his complete absorption. The way he was purposefully manipulating his finger made me vaguely uncomfortable and gave me a sense of foreboding.

In retrospect, I can see that the state of mind that had been evoked in me was one of anxious anticipation. It was like being held in a kind of unwilling trance by this man's strange performance. Then the finger emerged and I suddenly, but too late, understood the nature of my discomfort. He had collected a truly huge piece of mucus. Looking me straight in the eye for the first time, he matter-of-factly sucked it into his mouth and swallowed it.

My reaction was impossible to contain. I felt an intense urge to vomit. I lost control of my facial expression. Every iota of the disgust and revulsion I was feeling must have been visible at that moment. Still looking me in the eye, only now with an unmistakable expression of triumph and satisfaction, the patient calmly stood up and left the room.

The power of this memory is such that even now, many years later, I can feel the intrusive control this man exercised over my internal state. I remember sitting alone in the interview room and being flooded with feelings of disgust, loathing, and shame. In my mind, I avenged myself by imagining the patient rotting away on the chronic ward of a filthy state hospital. I could see that his previous therapists were correct; he was hopeless, he deserved his fate. At the same time, I was deeply shocked by the intensity of my hatred. How could I harbor such venom toward my own patient? How was it that I was over-reacting so massively to such a trivial incident?

I wish I could say that I eventually worked over my reaction and was able to resume a therapeutic stance. In those days, I knew almost nothing about projective identifications. In any event, information alone probably would not have sufficed to help me withstand the intensity of Mr. C.'s destructiveness. He had succeeded in causing me to share an experience of loathing and alienation that was beyond my capacity to contain.

The corrosive hatred I felt for a relatively few moments was the staple of this man's inner world. My inability to survive and remain effective in the face of his attack must have confirmed his belief in his malignancy. He clearly took omnipotent pride in making me hate him, thereby defeating my effort to be helpful. In a sense, he was demonstrating his omnipotence each time he committed an act of willful psychological suicide, vengefully cutting himself adrift from human connectedness.

The two cases that follow also involve evocations of hatred. In both, the staff rejected and punished patients who had committed acts that were shocking and repellent. Each of these patients was probably capable of being drawn into an alliance, but the staff's revulsion was of such proportions as to preclude working together.

A schizophrenic woman, during a period of delusional agitation, had attempted to harm her two small children.

Fortunately, they escaped injury and were subsequently placed in the home of a relative. The woman was committed for psychiatric treatment. On the ward, she showed no apparent concern for her children. Her lack of guilt provoked hatred and aggression among the ward staff. It was only with some difficulty that the outward signs of professionalism were maintained.

The feelings of outrage found a number of more or less disguised and ego-syntonic discharge channels. Severe and unnecessarily punitive restrictions were placed on the woman's activities long after her psychosis had lifted and she had ceased to present a danger to anyone. When she protested that she did not deserve such harsh treatment, her commitment papers were taken from the chart and the details of her abuse of the children were read to her in a tone of sadistic satisfaction and self-vindication.

The patient's need to assert her innocence elicited in the staff a corresponding need to prove to her that she was getting exactly what she deserved. The staff's identification with her sadistic superego precursors perpetuated the patient's inability to acknowledge the guilt as her own.

Similar milieu dynamics can be seen in the case of another schizophrenic patient, a young man committed to a forensic hospital. This patient had killed his father during a period of paranoid psychosis. Although he had been treated with neuroleptic medication for several years, his psychosis had only partially subsided and he remained consciously unaware of having killed his father. When questioned, he adamantly denied responsibility and slipped into delusional explanations to account for the death.

In addition to his medication, the patient received a form of psychotherapy best characterized as aggressive reality indoctrination. His social worker and therapist were determined that he would acknowledge and show remorse for his crime. Their sessions with him consisted mainly of various threats and inducements to persuade him to confess. Part of the process included reading and/or paraphrasing the commitment papers and police reports to force the patient to understand the overwhelming evidence against him. His inability to do so was viewed in moral rather than psychological terms. In the eyes of his therapists, the patient continued to be reprobate.

One could speculate about the nature of the anxiety evoked by the patricide. Whatever the specifics may have been, it was obvious that both therapists had distanced themselves from the patient and from any sense of working with him. Far from being stubbornly unwilling to confess, he was in a state of constant and unbearable panic. His denial of reality—continually on the verge of failing—was all that kept him from being plunged into suicidal guilt. The more his therapists sought acknowledgment and remorse, the more they elicited denial and delusional defenses, which further fueled their outrage.

These two rather extreme examples dramatically illustrate the extent to which the boundary between treatment and punishment may become blurred. In the absence of a strong commitment to a therapeutic alliance, this crucial distinction becomes even more tenuous. It should also be noted that relating to patients as criminal offenders functions as a compromise formation: vengefulness is discharged via the superego but the "badness" is experienced as residing exclusively in the criminal/patient.

One might object that the two patients just discussed were indeed guilty of criminal conduct for which they would have been harshly punished had they not been mentally ill. What conceivable therapeutic purpose is served by failing to confront them with their guilt? If the purpose of therapy is to foster a greater acceptance of reality, perhaps it was important and necessary to remind them of what they had done.

These questions are often heard on the ward and it is not

difficult to identify with the outrage that fuels them. Such feelings contribute to the tendency to extrapolate concepts, methods, and values from the field of criminal justice and apply them in psychiatric settings. The shift to a criminal justice stance could be characterized as a type of role confusion in which therapists become agents of social control and punishment, as described by Szasz.

However, the Szaszian perspective neglects the transference/countertransference dimension. In the two cases just noted, staff members found themselves possessed of an urgent need to attack and punish. They were unable to contain their rage and guilt, just as neither patient had been able to contain rage and guilt. The ensuing enactments of loathing and cruelty can be seen as a form of reciprocal psychological regulation in which patients rid themselves of internally attacking superego precursors and staff-enacted identifications with these projected components via sadistic treatment interventions. The social control perspective passes over this whole subterranean world of primitive affect and unconscious transaction.

Representing Reality

The therapists in both cases above believed it was their duty to represent reality. This notion is frequently misunderstood and misapplied. All too often, it is taken as mandating a confrontational stance, thus feeding into enactment potentials.

When patients are assaulted with the knowledge that they are sick or that their conduct is inappropriate, they tend to reject the message as well as the messenger. A familiar constellation of fears, fantasies, and delusional defenses becomes reinforced: the therapist is plotting with family members, is attempting to take over their mind, is trying to turn them into a homosexual, to poison them, and so forth. These delusions capture the noxious and intolerable nature of the reality the therapist is attempting to inculcate.

Helping regressed patients accept and truly integrate reality can only take place within a larger psychological context, requiring work with a complex matrix of structural and dynamic tensions and balances. By focusing on the factors that contribute to the loss of reality, the therapist aligns himself with the patient's threatened ego in a manner that invites active collaboration.

During the course of this work, there are usually long periods during which the therapist deliberately refrains from contradicting the patient's more or less psychotic reality. Instead, he allows himself to experience trial immersions in the matrix of primitive tensions that sustain the loss of reality. By exposing himself to the most regressed and bizarre sectors of the patient's subjectivity, he becomes vulnerable to powerful anxieties that test his stamina and, at times, his courage. During these moments, the temptation to prematurely represent reality becomes particularly intense.

In addition to countertransference factors, the therapist is typically subjected to social and institutional inducements to prematurely and authoritatively represent reality. It is often difficult to resist succumbing, as these pressures offer a sanctioned escape route from the disturbing emotional impact of therapeutic engagement.

A tactful, respectful, and nonconfrontational therapeutic stance does not imply acceptance of delusions and distortions. It does, however, imply acceptance of the patient's need, at least for the moment, to be deluded. Within this context, the therapist remains continually alert for opportunities to help expand sectors of observing ego, of accurate reality testing, and of more mature and adaptive modes of defense. A strategic sense of timing and an accurate empathy for the quality and degree of the patient's anxiety are of the essence in this work. Clumsy or premature interpretations can set back weeks or months of painstaking effort.

Misalliances

When the therapeutic alliance is neglected or insufficiently understood and valued, certain characteristic misalliances are more likely to ensue. I will close this chapter with four vignettes in which therapists or other staff members were drawn into inappropriate entanglements with persons outside the hospital, essentially functioning as agents of those persons. In each case, the misalliance was justified in therapeutic terms. However, in effect, staff members allowed themselves to become participants in the countertransference enactments of the outside parties.

In the first case, a ward staff unconsciously participated in a father's pathogenic sexual intrusiveness with his psychotic daughter. This attractive but deeply confused woman in her mid-thirties was brought to the hospital by her elderly father. His petition described at some length her apparently irrational promiscuity.

The father had involved himself in some of the most intimate details of the daughter's sexuality. Because he was preoccupied with the fear that she would become pregnant, he demanded to inspect her undergarments each month to determine if she had begun her menses. He also searched her room looking for condoms or birth control pills and he examined her bed linens. He was also in the habit of dramatically interrupting her visits to male friends to rescue her.

The patient's central delusion, which had been deeply entrenched for many years, was that she was involved in a passionate but stormy love affair with a clergyman many years her senior. In talking with her, it soon became clear that she was as preoccupied with her father as he was with her. Her apparently random and indiscriminate sexual behavior was in fact unconsciously designed to tantalize him and cause him intolerable jealousy. It was also experienced as a sort of declaration of emancipation from the suffocating intimacy demanded by the father.

The patient's sexual history was elaborated in great detail during the father's numerous conversations with various staff members. He soon became a fixture on the ward, always present during visiting hours and remaining long afterward to apprise the staff of his views on his daughter's treatment.

Increasingly, he expressed anxiety about certain details of the ward. Why were men and women housed on the same unit? What efforts were being made to monitor his daughter's behavior on the midnight shift? How would the staff determine if she was secretly having sexual contacts? Clearly, he needed and expected the staff to function as a narcissistic extension, omnipotently monitoring and controlling all aspects of the daughter's sexuality in his absence and blocking any movement toward greater individuation.

The father badgered the staff unceasingly; his anxious preoccupation was almost palpable. The staff found it increasingly difficult to formulate routine management arrangements without his interference. For example, he demanded the right to veto all passes from the hospital, since the daughter might use unsupervised time to secretly meet with a boyfriend.

The staff initially experienced the father as annoying and more than a little strange. But the attractive and seductive daughter stirred up feelings that were very troubling. Gradually, an implicit alliance between father and staff evolved. The result was that management decisions became unusually restrictive, taking on a quality of anxiety, infantilization, and intrusiveness.

This alliance was perceived by the patient as confirming her experience of the father as ubiquitous, omnipotent, and suffocating. Staff members became his poorly differentiated extensions. To protect herself from impending merger with the father/staff, she became increasingly oppositional and unreachable. As a result of her stay on the ward, the sexualized symbiotic relationship with her father was more deeply entrenched than before.

A local businessman whose paranoid son had insulted, threatened, and defied him for many years, was almost entirely unaware of his murderous rage toward the very difficult and provocative son. When the son's condition periodically deteriorated, he would arrange for hospitalization with the help of a therapist with whom he had become friendly over the years. The therapist would threaten the son with commitment if he refused to accept private hospitalization. The businessman experienced intense satisfaction and vicarious triumph as the son submitted to the therapist's authority.

During the course of a paranoid regression, the son was admitted to a state hospital after having been petitioned by his father. Although he preferred to remain where he was, the father arranged a transfer to the private facility, where he would again be under the care of the father's friend. The patient was convinced that his father had again turned the tables on him and that he was once more under the father's vengeful control.

In his dealings with the therapist, the patient remained suspicious and ingratiating. He was unable to establish a trusting relationship with any member of the treatment team. He saw his admission as justifying the need to sadistically control the dangerous father. For his part, the therapist was happy to use his professional status to provide a favor for a friend in need. He seemed to have no awareness of being enlisted in an enactment of the father's aggression.

The proprietress of a small group care home where several formerly hospitalized schizophrenic men resided persuaded a hospital therapist to supply her with neuroleptic medication in liquid concentrate form. It seemed that certain boarders were refusing their tablets. She felt anxious that they would "start to act up." Her plan was to maintain order by surreptitiously adding concentrates to the morning juice or cereal.

Concentrates were ordinarily not available outside the hospital. The foster mother was able to prevail upon the therapist because he shared her belief that medication had to be maintained at all costs. Both viewed psychiatric patients as lacking the capacity for independent judgment and regarded the deception as dictated by the patients' best interest.

Perhaps the most striking consideration in this case was that no individual clinical assessments were thought to be necessary. Apparently, it was inconceivable that any of the men were refusing their medication for reasons deserving of examination. By medicating them without even a cursory assessment, the therapist participated in an aggressive devaluation.

It is important to appreciate the resonances likely to be set in motion in schizophrenic patients by the secret induction of mind-altering substances and by the deception and betrayal of caretakers. The treatment approach of the therapist and foster mother supported the most malignant persecutory assumptions about the nature of human relations. Dealing with these patients as poorly balanced neurochemical entities was an anxiety-reducing reflex; neither participant was even vaguely aware of the deeply hostile implications of the treatment intervention.

In the next case, it is possible to report in much greater detail a complex interplay between transference enactment and countertransference misalliance. The case involves a hospital administrator and a social worker from an outside agency who combined to attack a provocative patient, thus enacting split-off sadistic elements of the patient's primitive objects. It also involves a therapist who unconsciously lived out the idealized polarity of the patient's inner world.

The patient, Ms. T., was a manic-depressive woman who had been treated by her state hospital therapist, Dr. A., through a series of admissions over several years (see

Chapter 4). Ms. T. had carried on a long feud with a child protection worker who suspected she was neglecting her young son. During periods of psychosis, the patient abused and threatened the worker. As a result, the worker had become almost as angry and vindictive as the patient.

During the course of one hospitalization, Ms. T. could frequently be overheard on the ward telephone, screaming the vilest accusations at the worker, who was considering taking custody of her son. However, when the psychosis subsided after a few weeks, she began to make relatively calm and reasonable plans for a day pass to visit the worker at her office, to try to convince her that the son was receiving adequate care.

Needless to say, the worker experienced considerable trepidation when Ms. T. told her of her intention to visit. She immediately phoned Dr. A. to question whether a pass should be allowed. When it became clear that he saw no reason to prevent it, the worker contacted a hospital administrator who she hoped would overrule him. The administrator, who knew the patient by reputation, had great reservations about allowing her out of the hospital. But since it seemed unlikely that she would harm anyone and since she had important business to conduct, Dr. A. declined to cancel the pass.

A day or two after Ms. T. returned from the pass—which she reported to have gone well—Dr. A. received an angry but also somewhat triumphant call from the administrator. She had been contacted again by the child protection worker who told her, in evident distress, that Ms. T. had come to the office and caused a chaotic and outrageous scene. According to the administrator, the patient had been agitated, threatening, and was rolling around on the floor. She had eventually been bodily expelled from the building by security personnel. The administrator made it clear that she would henceforth be monitoring the case to prevent further ill-considered passes.

Feeling that he had been misled by the patient, Dr. A. experienced an urge to aggressively interrogate her and to clamp down very hard on her future movements. By the next session, however, he felt sufficiently in control of his sense of betrayal to factually and calmly relate the conversation with the administrator. The patient appeared to be as surprised and upset as he was by the administrator's account of her behavior.

According to Ms. T., when she arrived at the child protection agency she was told that her worker was out of the building and was advised to return at a later date. Instead, she went to the office of the worker's supervisor and persuaded him to listen to her complaints about the manner in which her case was being handled. This gentleman had apparently promised to look into the situation and, with his assurances in mind, Ms. T. left the building. She pleaded with Dr. A. to accept her version of these events and not believe her capable of lying to him after their years of working together. She also begged him not to cancel her future passes.

The therapist left this session feeling, if anything, more confused than before. It was apparent that he had to resolve the conflicting versions of Ms. T.'s behavior. She had urged him to contact the supervisor, who would expose the lies of the worker who hated her and wanted to prevent her from receiving passes. He immediately phoned the supervisor, who verified the patient's story in all essential details. Dr. A. felt relieved, as though personally vindicated. He then realized he had been somewhat surprised to learn that his patient was apparently not guilty of outrageous behavior, as charged.

Dr. A. now believed the social worker to be the real culprit in this tangled web of false accusations and misinformation. He phoned her, fully expecting to hear her claim that Ms. T. had been agitated, threatening, rolling on the floor, and so forth. However, while she made little effort to disguise her dislike—which had been intensified when Ms. T. appealed to her supervisor—she related an account of events similar to what had previously been related by the patient and the supervisor. However, she added certain crucial details.

The worker noted that she had informed the hospital administrator that Ms. T. had been "roaming the floor" at the agency and had never suggested she was "rolling on the floor." Nor had she stated that the patient had been agitated or threatening. Furthermore, she could not imagine how the administrator had understood her to say that Ms. T. was escorted from the building by security guards. As far as she could recall, she had mentioned that her supervisor had walked the patient to the door following their conversation.

It now finally became apparent that the source of the accusations lay not in what had been said but in what had been heard. The hospital administrator, who was ready to believe Ms. T. capable of almost any outrage, had massively distorted the meaning of her conversation with the child protection worker in a manner that confirmed her devalued image of psychiatric patients in general and Ms. T. in particular.

Knowing this administrator as he had for many years, Dr. A. was not too surprised to learn that she had transformed "roaming the floor" into "rolling on the floor," or that an ordinary walk to the door had been understood as an ejection by security personnel. These misperceptions were probably facilitated by the accusatory tone of the protection worker, who was completely unable to disguise her dislike of Ms. T. Despite their differences over details, the worker and the administrator experienced an unconscious connectedness: both needed to use the hospital to attack and/or omnipotently control the patient.

The patient was an active participant in this misalliance. She had for years created hatred, confusion, and upheaval both inside and outside the hospital. Her cruelest weapon was her astuteness in intuiting the vulnerabilities of those around her and in mercilessly attacking them in the most sadistic fashion. Dislike of her had developed to the point that many nurses and aides openly groaned and made hateful remarks in her presence when she came for admission. Some staff members blamed Dr. A. because—as they perceived the situation—he allowed her to use the hospital to escape the consequences of her obnoxious and irresponsible behavior. It was clear that many wanted to see her roasted in her own juices.

For many years, the patient's admissions were characterized by active splitting of the milieu. She experienced nurses and other ward staff as mistreating her. All of their attempts to establish themselves as good caretakers were undermined and defeated. For many, it became difficult not to hate a patient who devoted herself to the tireless destruction of all their efforts to be helpful.

In her relationship with her therapist, however, Ms. T. was syrupy sweet, coy, girlish, seductive, and idealizing. His assigned task was to protect her from the hateful and envious ward staff. This splitting continued for several admissions, during which Dr. A. remained unaware of the extent to which he was playing out a role from her primitive fantasies.

He had been shocked and surprised by the harshness of his feelings toward Ms. T. when informed of the scene at the child protection agency. He also remembered the surprise he felt when he discovered she was actually innocent. He began to wonder if he had ever fully understood the depth of pain, hatred, and vindictiveness she evoked in those around her, especially among his co-workers.

As he became able to consider the possibility that he had been actively fostering and enjoying the patient's idealizations, Dr. A. tightened up certain aspects of the therapeutic frame that he had permitted to become much too blurred and indulgent. About this same time, certain key processes within the milieu began to shift. Perhaps most significantly, co-workers increasingly expressed understandable derivatives of the split during team meetings. This development was described in detail in Chapter 4.

In a pivotal therapy session, it became clear to Dr. A. that in relinquishing the idealizing transference, he was giving up a posture that insulated him from his patient's destructiveness. In this session, Ms. T. shifted without warning or transition from her customary seductive/helpless mode. With delusional intensity and with an almost total loss of observing ego, she experienced Dr. A. as the malignant, exploiting, greedy, and rejecting maternal figure who was personally responsible for all the injuries and losses she had suffered since childhood.

During that session and the ones to follow, Ms. T. bellowed and pounded and was close to physically attacking Dr. A. However, she kept on her own side of the heavy wood table in the consultation room. Even at the height of her psychotic rage, she needed to protect and preserve Dr. A. Eventually, the rage would run its course and she would experience a few moments of profound and wrenching grief during which she became remarkably lucid and sane. During those brief moments, she experienced in the transference the mother she hated and wanted to destroy and the mother she inexpressibly loved and yearned for as one.

The sadistic vengefulness Ms. T. provoked externalized a split-off experience of her mother, as distorted through the lens of her own rage. The readiness of others to identify with and enact this cruel and devaluing part-object was apparent on the ward and also in the alliance forged between the hospital administrator and the child protection worker.

Dr. A. had, for a number of years, distanced himself from the primitive attacking component of Ms. T.'s internal world. It was not until the events described here that he was able to experience—via the countertransference—the depth and intensity of his patient's destructive rage.

6

The Bureaucracy

The treatment milieu typically exists within a complex matrix of administrative rules, regulations, and procedures, some designed to meet in-house needs and others to bring the hospital into compliance with a vast array of mandates generated by powerful regulatory agencies and third-party payers. In many instances, the functional relationship between a regulation and its intended beneficial clinical outcome is quite clear, but this is not always or necessarily the case. In certain of the hospital settings examined here, the regulatory agenda had taken on a life of its own, occupying a position of primacy even when manifestly injurious to the mission of providing treatment.

I refer to this state of affairs as *bureaucratization* to distinguish it conceptually from conventional administrative practice. In actuality, the two modes of administration may shade into one another and it is not always clear exactly where to draw the boundary. Bureaucratization is of interest clinically because it tends to encourage a characteristic manner of relating to patients, co-workers, and the treatment endeavor as a whole. Most often, this involves a shift in the direction of power-oriented interpersonal relationships, an emphasis on appearance over substance, and an anxiety-driven need to avoid blame and the assumption of personal responsibility. In the realm of countertransference dynamics, bureaucratization both disguises and provides institutionally sanctioned channels for the enactment of dehumanization, splitting, and various forms of omnipotence.

The material in this chapter is drawn almost entirely from state hospital settings because it is in this hospital system that bureaucratized administrative practice seems to have reached its most advanced stage and where its interaction with countertransference factors can be most clearly observed. The discussion focuses on organizational arrangements that exacerbate splitting and distancing, disrupt the team's containment capacities, and support power-oriented forms of relatedness.

Within this context, the impact of bureaucratic micromanagement is examined. Growing in part out of a profound mistrust of personal and professional autonomy and an obsessive need to control persons and events, the micromanagement orientation almost invariably results in a heightened reliance on excessive monitoring and coercive supervisory methods, massively altering the character of work and relatedness in the treatment milieu and shifting the balance between containment and enactment.

CENTRALIZATION AND SPLITTING

Regressed patients exert a powerful interpersonal pull for part-object identifications and enactments. When team members can contain and psychologically process these enactment potentials, an appropriate clinical response is more likely to ensue. However, the pull may exert its effects beyond the confines of the team and the ward, drawing in persons not directly involved in the clinical work. This results in added complications, usually not favorable for the containment process.

In bureaucratized settings, boundaries between administrative and clinical functions tend to be blurred, inviting intrusions by off-ward personnel. In some instances, team members may actively solicit the intervention of administrators. Such intrusions can often be understood as enactments by proxy of a specific countertransference impulse or defense that the team or team member was unable to contain.

When enactment-inducing tensions can be held within the milieu, they are subject to the potentially corrective influence of ongoing clinical experience. In addition, since staff members work together in close proximity, they may be able to reestablish relatively open lines of communication even after having been split into factions. In contrast, off-ward administrators tend to intervene on the basis of relatively minimal or distorted information that has been filtered through the experience of one segment of the staff. Many are isolated in their respective fiefdoms and are unaware of the transference/countertransference tensions that elicited their involvement. Perhaps most importantly, they may see problems on the ward from a hierarchical, power-based perspective, thus feeding into already present tendencies to deal with primitive tensions by means of aggression-saturated interventions.

Administrative involvement in the milieu may also bring with it extraneous conflicts and rivalries. Splits in the clinical staff usually become intractable when linked up with power struggles among off-ward factions. While team processes can be used to integrate splitting confined to the milieu (see Chapter 4), there seems to be no effective way to reintegrate once disputes are taken up as ammunition in off-ward conflicts or to support some other aspect of the bureaucratic agenda.

A student therapist had been considering a pass for a young man, Mr. H., who had been hospitalized on numerous occasions. The patient had recompensated from the psychotic symptoms present at admission and was now functioning at his usual level of moderate character pathology. The hospital was an acute care facility, where standard practice was to discharge patients like Mr. H. to outpatient clinics as soon as their condition permitted. Encouraging Mr. H. to resume taking care of certain practical matters outside the hospital was the last step before his discharge.

While the student was assessing the patient's condition, the social worker who usually worked with the team had to be away for several days and a substitute was temporarily assigned. During a team meeting, the substitute worker noted that the patient, whom she knew from previous admissions, was functioning remarkably well. The student and the staff psychiatrist later reviewed the team's discussion, including the social worker's comments, and decided to allow a pass, although a pass had not been specifically discussed during the meeting.

When the social worker was later told of the pass, she seemed surprised and offended. She brought up the patient's history of alcohol abuse and noted that he had once been struck by a car while intoxicated. She did not allude to having been left out of the decision-making process, but focused entirely on the potential dangers of the proposed pass. Feeling somewhat uncomfortable, the student consulted with her clinical supervisor, but failed to mention that the pass had not been explicitly discussed in the team meeting. Since the patient clearly met the usual criteria for passes, the supervisor advised the student not to alter the plan.

At this point, it becomes difficult to disentangle events, in part because of backstage maneuvering and also because of the number of people who became involved.

The evening before the scheduled pass, the director of social work phoned the student's supervisor to complain that the pass was clinically inappropriate. She also stated, parenthetically, that she was incensed that the social worker had not been sufficiently consulted. The supervisor, now aware of the hurt feelings that were feeding into this impasse, agreed that his student had been remiss. He promised to contact the student in the morning and instruct her to review the situation with the entire team before proceeding with the pass.

When he arrived in the morning, the supervisor was surprised to find the situation in a state of confusion. The social work director had spoken with Dr. M., the director of inpatient services, and persuaded him to cancel the pass. Dr. M. did not consult with any of the clinical staff involved in the patient's care and overlooked the fact that a team meeting was scheduled in an hour or two in which the situation was to be reviewed. The supervisor's impression was that Dr. M. was responding to intense pressure from the director of social work, who had important connections in the hospital hierarchy and who was obviously determined to make her influence felt in this situation.

The supervisor, by now incensed at the manner in which the process had unfolded, complained to the hospital's administrators. The next day, he and the student were summoned to a meeting. After a few introductory comments, the cordial atmosphere quickly deteriorated. It soon became clear that everyone involved felt personally threatened and angry. Given the intensity of feelings, there could be no real attempt to sort out the events of the past few days.

From the perspective of administrators, the principal issue was the perceived challenge to their necessary and legitimate prerogatives. Thus, the supervisor's demand for clearer boundaries between administrative and clinical functions received an angry and uncomprehending reception. Given the emotional climate of the meeting, it was probably experienced as a personal affront by many of those present. In the end, supervisor and student were told in no uncertain terms that administrators would intervene in clinical matters whenever, in their judgment, it was deemed necessary.

Tensions among team members become essentially unresolvable when outsiders with turfs to defend and agendas to pursue are drawn into the process. In this instance, there were complications that increased the likelihood of off-ward involvement. Had the therapist informed her supervisor that she failed to consult the social worker, he might have realized that something was amiss much sooner. The fact that the social worker was a temporary substitute who was not integrated into team functions was another exacerbating factor.

It may also be interesting to note that everyone involved in this dispute gravitated to a more extreme position in reaction to feelings of personal threat. The supervisor—angry that his counsel had been pre-empted—was unable to present his complaint in a conciliatory manner that might have elicited greater sympathy. For their part, administrators found themselves in the position of denying the need for even modest guidelines to govern interventions. In this manner, a relatively tractable problem grew into a bitter and deeply troubling conflict that was likely to have further untoward ramifications in the future.

The patient's pass had been precipitously cancelled. He was told only that further review was needed. The fact that the pass was a source of conflict among team members could not fail to have been apparent, but he could only guess at the details. The erratic manner in which promises were made and broken certainly could not have inspired him with much trust or confidence.

However, he was allowed to go a few days later, and this time there was no interference, despite the fact that his condition had not changed. Administrators had apparently made their point and further interventions were not necessary. The patient handled the pass well and was discharged soon afterward.

The next example also involves a split that was amplified and distorted by off-ward administrators. In this case, however, there is reason to believe that the patient was actively involved in the process.

The incident began in a ward community meeting, when a patient began without warning to exhibit dramatic and alarming behavior. He falteringly rose from his chair in a sort of fugue state and began to stumble around the room, trembling violently and mumbling incoherently. His eyes were glassy and he seemed ready to collapse at any moment. The staff was alarmed, fearing he might be undergoing a dangerous medical crisis.

A ward psychiatrist was present and attempted to examine the patient as the rest of the staff looked on anxiously. Apparently, his response was experienced by some of those present as ambiguous and unsatisfactory. Later, in a team meeting, certain staff members expressed feelings of helplessness. A nurse stated she had felt abandoned by the psychiatrist.

This remark was important because it signaled the possibility that a primitive part-object identification had been evoked in the nurse. The patient's dramatic helplessness and distress may have drawn her into a self-experience that he could enact but not otherwise express.

The prognosis for exploring and clarifying the patient's behavior and its impact on the staff was not initially unfavorable. The nurse had described her reaction as a subjective feeling state; she did not accuse the psychiatrist of actual abandonment. However, no one present recognized the significance of her experience, and the meeting eventually moved on to other topics.

The patient was later examined by a hospital internist who agreed with the psychiatrist that the symptoms were probably psychological in origin. That seemed to end the matter. The feelings voiced in the team meeting were not elaborated or pursued in subsequent discussions.

However, a couple of weeks later, it became known that someone in the state Department of Mental Health had been informed of what transpired in the community meeting and had initiated an informal inquiry to determine if the distressed patient had received inadequate care. Although it was quickly determined that there were no grounds to pursue the matter, the psychiatrist was deeply offended. He accused the nurse of making the complaint. She strongly denied the accusation.

At this point, there was an almost total breakdown of the team process. The most serious breach was the decision to carry an emotionally charged issue to off-ward bureaucrats without first having given the team a fair chance to clarify and resolve it. It was never revealed how the complaint reached the Department of Mental Health. However, in response to the first breach, others inevitably followed. The aggrieved psychiatrist took the matter to the hospital director, Dr. R., who decided to deal with it himself.

Dr. R. faced a situation that required skillful and sensitive intervention. Even with the most careful handling, it is far from clear that the damage done to the team could be repaired. However, Dr. R. was not primarily concerned with the split in the team. He angrily accused the nurse of maliciously attacking a physician and threatened her with dire consequences if he could prove she made the complaint. For Dr. R., the issue was whether nurses were permitted to criticize physicians.

The nursing director resented Dr. R. and competed with him at every opportunity. She also felt she had turf to defend. She experienced his tirade against the staff nurse as a veiled personal attack on her and an attempt to put the nursing department in its place. She too was uninterested in the clinical origins and implications of the split. As the battle was joined on both sides, rivalries and anxieties that had simmered beneath the surface for years increasingly crowded the clinical situation out of the picture.

INTRUSION, SURVEILLANCE, COERCION

Bureaucracies tend to react to unregulated behavior as inherently threatening. In my years on the wards, I saw little to persuade me that mental health bureaucrats are less susceptible to this outlook than others. The traditional notion of professionalism, with its emphasis on internalized standards of competence, personal responsibility, and respect for the privacy of personal relationships, is especially likely to elicit a mixture of condescension and alarm. In the state hospital system, absorbing professional practice into the fabric of monitored, regulated, and controlled activities seemed to be a prime focus of the bureaucratic agenda.

The involvement of off-ward personnel in clinical matters—whether through mandates designed to shape practice or through intervention in individual cases—may exert tremendous pressures on clinicians to think and work in a manner consistent with bureaucratic values. Not infrequently, depersonalized, power-oriented modes of dealing with human problems are imported to the ward and are enlisted in support of distancing and omnipotent control. For many staff members, micromanagement becomes a model for clinical interactions with patients. As a result, it becomes difficult at times to clearly differentiate therapeutic from bureaucratic activities.

A state hospital administrator, Mr. S., established a uniform policy on phone calls during ward community meetings after receiving complaints that meetings on a certain ward were continually interrupted by patients leaving the room to answer or make calls. He proposed to deal with the problem by disconnecting telephones on all wards during community meetings.

Patients on the ward in question were leaving meetings as part of a devaluing attack on their therapy and therapists. Staff members felt hurt and angry as patients repeatedly walked out of the group room to hold animated conversations with persons they were apparently more interested in talking with. The staff's appeal to Mr. S. was an attempt to regain control and discharge anger.

Mr. S. was inclined to oblige. He viewed the behavior in the community meeting as a challenge to be defeated by superior force. By administrative fiat, his plan would effectively transform an interesting and potentially productive clinical problem into an exercise in hierarchical control. Thus, an important channel for the expression and processing of highly charged derivatives would be effectively blocked.

The staff's decision to reach outside the ward illustrates how hospital administrators and procedures are enlisted in the service of countertransference defense. The image of the disconnected telephone vividly captures the disengagement from clinical processes on the ward in question. At no time during the period when patients were migrating in and out of meetings were team members able to make clinical use of the painful feelings of devaluation being evoked in them. Their acting out discharged anger, bypassed psychological processing, and supported the defensive transformation of an internal conflict into an interpersonal one.

The decision to appeal to Mr. S. for assistance tended to draw staff members into the role of lower echelon regulators who managed patients as administrators managed subordinates. In bureaucratized settings, there is often a great deal of more or less explicit pressure on staff to assume this posture. In contrast, clinicians who practice in a manner that supports optimal autonomy and responsible collaboration may be seen as challenging the ethos of control, thus evoking conflict with hospital bureaucrats.

The tension between therapists attempting to preserve islands of autonomous professional activity and bureaucrats seeking to advance the agenda of regulation was at times quite pronounced in the state hospital system. In some facilities, the relationship had taken on a mistrustful adversarial tone. Monitoring and regulation had advanced to a degree that they might more accurately have been characterized as surveillance and coercion. Compliance with mandates was enforced by intimidation and punishment. These conditions of work increasingly set the tone of interpersonal relatedness in the milieu. Their impact could hardly fail to be noticed by patients and interpreted as confirming that the external world was governed by the same hostile and manipulative forces they feared in themselves.

BUREAUCRATIC PRESENCE IN TREATMENT RELATIONSHIPS

One might suppose that bureaucratic intrusions, whatever their effect on other aspects of ward business, are easily barred from the privacy of the consulting room. In my experience, the opposite is more nearly the case. Whether clinicians take part in management functions (such as decisions on admission, discharge, passes, medication, etc.) or attempt to maintain a more classical stance of technical neutrality, their ability to isolate the therapeutic interaction from institutional pressures is extremely limited.

It is not uncommon for patients to report dreams or fantasies suggesting an awareness of external influence. I recall, for example, a session in which a student therapist repeatedly interrupted his patient's train of thought in order to extract information that was supposed to be entered in the chart. In the next session, the patient reported a dream in which he and the therapist were in the grip of an invisible electrical current. The intuited presence of powerful alien forces elicited heightened mistrust, withdrawal, persecutory defenses, and a blurring of boundaries.

This interaction also highlights the contrasting functions of information from bureaucratic and clinical perspectives. Since this contrast is crucial for understanding much of the material to follow, it may be helpful to define certain of its elements more explicitly.

From the bureaucratic point of view, factual information is needed to facilitate monitoring, accountability, planning, and regulation. In this frame of reference, the clinician may be regarded as simply another collector of data. The manner in which the data is obtained is less important than factors such as timeliness and completeness. Therapists who work under these conditions are under immense pressure to relate to patients as repositories of information.

In contrast, a clinical approach emphasizes the primacy of the unfolding human relationship within which information may come to light. In formulating questions, careful and respectful practice dictates a cautious assessment of a range of ego functions, including the state of the therapeutic alliance, the nature and intensity of currently activated anxieties, and the potential for decompensation. It is usually regarded as crucial to guard against an invasive or badgering approach; material is best allowed to emerge gradually as trust in the therapy develops. According to this way of working, information is regarded neither as an end in itself nor simply as a means to other more significant ends. Rather, it both facilitates and constitutes an essential expression of the patient's capacity to experience deeper and less anxious connectedness.

Paperwork Reality

Since the manifest purpose of regulation is to improve the quality of care, one might reasonably suppose that administrators and out-of-house auditors carefully observe the activities they regulate. In fact, they depend almost entirely on written material that is supposed to reflect and condense the realities of practice. Some regulators spend their entire careers immersed in a world of documents, many of which have only the most tenuous connection to events on the wards.

In certain of the settings described here, the world of regulation and documentation had acquired the status of a quasi-independent reality. Its often bizarre and destructive character transformed the nature of clinical practice in these settings.

The ostensible purpose of the psychiatric hospital is to provide effective treatment, but to the extent that it becomes bureaucratized, its "product" changes. An observer who examined daily work life at the state hospital I refer to here as Midtown Psychiatric Center (MPC) might fairly conclude that a primary purpose of its existence was to churn out paperwork. During the years of my tenure at MPC, the staff spent a steadily growing portion of its time and energy producing forms and documents intended to demonstrate compliance with bureaucratic regulations. Compliance and documentation gradually became obsessions, central points of reference in the hospital's collective consciousness.

Additional layers of paperwork were continually being generated to attest to the fact that existing layers had been attended to. The result was a self-referential system that was often completely out of touch with clinical reality. For example, when members of the staff complained that paperwork duties made it impossible to devote sufficient time to patients, new regulations were promulgated requiring minimal patient contact hours each week. Of course, to demonstrate compliance, additional time-consuming documents had to be completed.

Many staff members attended to paperwork in a perfunctory manner, resenting the added burden. Some resisted on principle. Others were ambivalent, but attempted to conscientiously serve two masters. Despite these differences, it was clear that the ideology and practice of paperwork could be seductive, lulling staff into a realm of detached stereotyped preoccupation. Bureaucrats, for their part, usually refrained from asking embarrassing questions so long as production was sustained.

At times, one had the impression of an unspoken collusion between those who complained of the added burden—but were unconsciously grateful for the disconnectedness it provided—and hospital bureaucrats, who tended to be consciously viewed as demanding taskmasters. I can attest from my own experience that those of us who were unhappy with paperwork duties were not always immune from using them as an institutionally sanctioned defensive activity. In contrast to certain other activities that provided needed rest and retreat, paperwork created an illusion of serious engagement while devaluing too-close connectedness with real patients.

Intimidation

Paperwork is generated in some significant measure out of devaluation and anxiety. The bureaucratic view of human nature seems to tend toward cynicism. This is especially evident on the question of whether staff members can be relied upon to conscientiously perform their duties if not constantly watched and in fear of sanction. Most typically, the answer seems to be a resounding no. Threats, inducements, and constant monitoring are felt to be necessary to ensure compliance and accountability.

I do not know if many bureaucrats actually believe that omnipotent control of human activity is possible and desirable, but it is remarkable how many act as though they do. Perhaps this state of affairs has to do with a work environment in which those in authority quickly learn to dread being held personally responsible for the actions of others. When inevitable lapses occur, they react with redoubled efforts to establish ubiquitous control.

However, since it is not possible to observe everyone at all times, forms and documents assume paramount importance. The urgency of the need for control is reflected in the magical efficacy attributed to the written record, as though paperwork could encompass and render predictable the human world of infinite possibility.

At MPC, bureaucrats showed remarkably little interest in the clinical effects of regulatory practices. Nor were the underlying goals and assumptions on which regulation was predicated often seriously discussed. Unquestioning compliance with paperwork mandates had increasingly become an end in itself. Any lapse in production activated monitoring and enforcement mechanisms that had proliferated throughout the hospital.

Every week, threatening memos went out from various administrators, auditors, and monitoring committees to all those who were delinquent in maintaining required forms and documents. If infractions failed to be corrected in a timely fashion, the aggressiveness of the memos was systematically increased.

The constant pressure had a clear impact on the manner in which staff members defined priorities and related to their patients. Bureaucratic aggressiveness created a residue of bad feeling that was often discharged within the milieu. In addition, it seemed to legitimize punitive and authoritarian clinical practices. The humiliation of being treated as an irresponsible child could be partially deflected by identifying with the aggressor.

The mirror quality of aggression against patients can be seen in the Special Management Plan used at MPC. This procedure was viewed as a necessary and helpful clinical intervention; few would have characterized it as a parallel form of the threatening memos received by staff. Yet the similarity of tone, content, and method was uncanny. It was as though the staff was now able to turn the tables, inflicting the same indignities it had suffered.

Special Management Plans were directed at patients whose behavior had not been controlled by other methods. In theory, they did not necessarily involve coercive threats; in practice, however, they almost invariably consisted of a list of infractions and a companion list of escalating punishments that the staff promised to administer if compliance was not forthcoming.

Management plans were presented in written form. Patients were supposed to sign them to acknowledge receipt; thus they could not later deny they had been forewarned. On some wards, patients were summoned to appear before the entire treatment team to be formally apprised of the consequences of their unacceptable behavior. This litigious adversarial manner of relating acquired a routinized quality, so that it became more and more difficult to distinguish coercive enactments from ordinary and accepted clinical practice.

AGGRANDIZEMENT OF PAPERWORK

The world of paperwork required periodic ritualistic exercises that were intended to demonstrate that effective treatment was taking place. The Mad Hatter quality of some of this activity can be seen in the "Staffing Needs Assessment Process" (SNAP), an annual survey conducted by the state Department of Mental Health to determine staffing and funding levels at hospitals in the state system.

SNAP was supposed to measure services actually provided. The process involved auditors who exhaustively tallied the number of clinical contacts and activities documented in the charts. If the tally was high, the hospital was presumed to be providing a high level of service and funding might be increased or at least maintained. If it was low, staff and funding could be cut.

MPC's tally was seldom low. For weeks prior to the survey, nurses, clinicians, and administrators were feverishly busy coaching one another in the subtleties of enhancing and embellishing the charts. The staff was repeatedly exhorted to document all contacts, even the most trivial. Definitions of clinical activities were stretched to inflate the tally. The pressure to make the hospital look good and to preserve jobs was incredible. In some departments, staff received instructions to document frequencies of contact that were clearly unrealistic if not deliberately deceptive.

During one SNAP survey, I quietly conducted my own informal study of therapists and social workers. In this small and less-than-random sample, all of the individuals questioned acknowledged they could not possibly provide the frequency of sessions they had been specifying in their treatment plans.

A similar situation held true for the nursing staff. During the time frame noted above, treatment plans indicated that each patient on the ward was receiving planned nursing interventions totaling about 10 hours per week, an amount apparently specified by the Department of Nursing. Administrators did not realize (they evidently hadn't counted the number of patients per nurse) that each nurse was on record as providing over 30 hours of planned interventions each week under this policy. This was clearly absurd. Constant meetings, paperwork, ward upkeep, and unplanned interventions made it unlikely that nurses could provide even a substantial fraction of 30 hours.

In short, SNAP measured the hospital's ability to collude with state regulators in promulgating a convenient illusion, to enact a cynical ritual, and to dispense mutual benefits. As a direct and observable consequence of these surveys, real patients and real clinical commitment were explicitly devalued. SNAP made it clear to staff at all levels that producing impressive charts was among the hospital's most urgent priorities.

The Treatment Plan

Another avenue by which bureaucratic methods and values entered the milieu was the Team Treatment Plan (TTP). The TTP was intended to help in formulating a comprehensive interdisciplinary treatment approach. It was also supposed to provide an ongoing measure of progress by recording changes in behavior and symptoms. However, as the material to follow will suggest, the TTP could also function to support distancing, omnipotent control, and dehumanization.

When the TTP was first introduced at MPC, an effort was made to draw patients into the process of identifying problems and goals. The effort was gradually abandoned by most teams in the hospital. The TTP process seemed to pull in an opposite direction, encouraging hierarchical interactions in which patients were treated as passive recipients of goals generated by the staff.

Working on predefined externally imposed goals warded off anxiety by ruling out in advance potentially threatening realms of thought and feeling. When used in this manner, the TTP process constituted a sort of auxiliary ego-defense for both patients and staff, helping to keep the treatment on a predictable, carefully demarcated path.

Eventually, the TTP came to function on most wards at MPC as a rationale and methodology for imposing appropriate behavior and for rejecting and devaluing symptomatic behavior. Based on my experience with similar treatment plans at other hospitals, it seems likely that the TTP did not gravitate in the direction I have described due to any peculiarity at MPC. Rather, the inner logic of the approach tends to reinforce always present potentials to react to countertransference-related impulses and anxieties in this manner.

The TTP required conceptualizing problems and goals in terms that were readily measurable. The procedure was simple and compelling: team members listed target symptoms, specified the degree to which each would be modified, assigned interventions to each team member, and formulated measurable criteria that would concretely indicate the degree to which goals had been accomplished. The most primitive and scientifically naive notions of observation and measurement were applied to this task, generating highly stereotyped and impoverished formulations in which patients tended to be portrayed as dehumanized mechanisms, to be regulated and fine tuned like any other inanimate object.

Criteria of progress typically included goals such as "no verbalization of delusions for two weeks" or "refrains from cursing his therapist." Verbalization (or the lack thereof) was a popular criterion because it was concrete and readily measurable. What the patient actually felt or thought was not as easy to ascertain. From the perspective of the TTP, it was immaterial so long as the patient kept it to himself. In this same vein, there were rarely references to the specific content of delusions or to the delusion's role in a patient's inner life.

In the case of withdrawn patients, a typical goal might specify that a patient was to attend 50 percent of activities. The needs served by the patient's withdrawal and the possible recklessness of pushing him prematurely into unwanted social contact was often outside the scope of the criterion. Whether social participation was motivated by genuine interest and reduced anxiety or constituted a response to various inducements or coercive measures was also of little apparent relevance.

Time frames and the degree of compliance were spelled out with obsessive and arbitrary exactitude, providing a pseudoscientific aura. No one could explain why 75 percent was chosen instead of, say, 65 percent as a criterion. In fact, the exact level was beside the point. The attraction of this methodology was that it supported an illusion of omnipotent control, an unconscious fantasy in which team members could experience themselves as powerful, detached, and in complete mastery of themselves and their patients.

The need to ward off primitive tensions was of such proportions that the TTP sometimes became invested with magical properties, resembling a form of sorcery in which persons are harmed or controlled by manipulating symbolic representations. I remember a co-worker who, unable to tolerate contact with a particularly bizarre and difficult patient, became preoccupied with making tiny adjustments in the TTP. These manipulations soothed him, despite the fact that they failed to have any noticeable impact on the patient.

The TTP methodology limited the quality, depth, and scope of therapeutic interactions. It offered a reassuringly rigid and allegedly scientific conception of human functioning and generated a system of monitoring and predictable progress. Unconsciously, it helped establish a sense of mastery and of emotional distance. Staff members who participated in the TTP process might still succeed in building sensitive and respectful therapeutic relationships with their patients, but these accomplishments were almost certainly in spite of the TTP.

The TTP procedure also cast a shadow over the workings of the treatment team. Increasingly, clinical meetings became bureaucratized, devoted to dreary and ritualized recitations of lifeless information needed to turn out treatment plans in assembly-line fashion. It was not easy to make a transition from this mode of interaction to one in which the team functioned as a responsive clinical instrument. As a result, the team's potential for funneling in, containing, and processing primitive projections was severely diminished.

Confidentiality

At the facilities surveyed here—both state and private— charts were freely accessible to the entire staff on the ward. In addition, they were read by secretaries, medical records clerks, various in-house and out-of-house auditors and accreditors, by attorneys representing patients in commitment hearings, by students rotating through the ward, and by hospital administrators. At private hospitals, data from the charts was made available to insurance representatives. I have also known of incidents in which information was furnished informally and without permission to patients' family members and to social service or law enforcement agencies.

A detailed examination of the limitations of confidentiality in hospital practice is beyond the scope of this book. My general view is that much of what appears in psychiatric charts meets legal, economic, and bureaucratic concerns, but that it is not necessarily clinically useful for much of it to appear in writing. From a strictly clinical perspective, the interdisciplinary team meeting is potentially a far more alive and helpful context for exchanging information among staff members. However, the discussion to follow will be narrowly focused, dealing primarily with the manner in which charting lends itself to misuse in hostile countertransference enactments.

Patients become willing to share information within the protective confines of a trusting relationship. As recipients of a special trust, therapists have a special obligation to protect confidentiality. Even the most cautious and discreet treatment note can be misused by one or another of the many persons who will read it. The result is that therapists may become unwitting co-actors in the betrayal of their patients.

An elderly depressed woman who was probably no longer capable of living independently had been hospitalized for several weeks, during which time she expressed great reluctance to giving up her apartment and moving to a home for the elderly. Although the proposed move seemed reasonable to the staff and had been suggested in a helpful spirit, she became anxious and depressed each time it was mentioned. It was clear that she experienced the move as putting her in a position of dependency and as signaling the approaching end of her life.

The staff's attitude shifted as the patient continued to resist the placement plan. Some became openly annoyed with what they took to be her stubbornness. Increasingly, one could hear hostile remarks about the manipulative quality of her physical complaints and of her refusal to accept an obvious reality. The annoyance probably had much to do with the staff's need to ward off guilt for inflicting injury on a woman whom everyone had grown fond of. The power struggle was in some way comforting because it created distance from the guilt.

One staff member, who was very invested in winning the tug of war, insisted to the patient in an irritated manner that she must recognize she was seriously depressed and cited as evidence a note in the chart written by her therapist. The note was quoted in a highly accusatory manner, as if to vanquish the patient's stubborn refusal to recognize reality once and for all. The patient was hurt and angered by this conversation and later told her therapist in no uncertain terms that she felt betrayed. Although she continued to try, she was not able to make much use of her therapy for the duration of her hospitalization.

Even the most innocuous comments, once committed to writing, are subject to violation and misuse that pass totally out of the therapist's control and draw him into unwanted participation in the enactments of co-workers. On the other hand, the therapist himself may use charting as an enactment channel. Overly informative and detailed notes may express an unconscious wish to injure and betray. Hostile impulses expressed in the chart may subsequently be picked up and amplified by other members of the staff who sense they are being invited to collude in attacking a patient.

A depressed alcoholic patient whose life was in a shambles used her therapy sessions to ritualistically repeat slogans and rules of living she had learned at Alcoholics Anonymous meetings. She desperately grasped for a reliable foothold to keep from slipping back into self-destructive drinking. The therapy frightened her badly because it felt as though her customary defenses were being even more eroded. In a sense, she was attempting to strengthen herself by orally incorporating magical words and phrases, just as she had attempted to accomplish with alcohol.

The therapist, without realizing it, had become frustrated with the patient's rejection of insight-oriented work. It seemed clear that his interpretations could not compete with the patient's preference for a magical cure and he felt increasingly angry, hurt, and impotent. Why, he wondered, did he put so much effort into trying to help his substance abusers, whose resistances seemed so deeply entrenched and unworkable?

A few days before the patient was scheduled to be discharged, the therapist noted in the chart that her rejection of insight left her vulnerable to a resumption of drinking under conditions of sufficient stress. He was vaguely aware he had been more specific and more willing to engage in prognostication than was his custom, but he did not give any thought to the hostile implications of his note.

The next day, however, as he was walking in the corridor, he was approached by the patient who was evidently in a state of near panic and barely controlled rage. She demanded to know why he had told the ward social worker that she would probably suffer a relapse and soon have to be readmitted. The therapist was stunned. He wanted to protest his innocence, but was unable to recall the details of his note from the day before. He believed he had not made specific predictions about relapse, but felt vaguely in the wrong nevertheless.

In re-examining the note and analyzing the emotional context in which it had been written, the therapist was able to untangle what had transpired. The note did seem to express a vengeful attack on the patient, although it indeed did not contain a specific prediction about relapse. The social worker, who was also evidently frustrated with the patient, had read the note and recognized the anger in it. He then amplified the attack in his own way. Thus, the patient's resistance had elicited a concerted countertransference enactment from at least two key members of the treatment team.

The use of charting as a mode of attack was particularly inviting in this case, since the hospital's demand for detailed progress notes provided a supportive rationale. If a sanctioned discharge channel had not been so readily available, a more productive struggle with the countertransference feelings might have ensued.

The treatment process is poorly served by the almost universal requirement that hospital therapists document their observations and assessments in the same manner as other staff members. Since this is unlikely to change in the current treatment climate, it is imperative that therapists assume responsibility for exercising caution and foresight. It is crucial, for example, that patients be clearly informed of the degree to which confidentiality can be provided. Also, although any note can be misused, some are inherently more inviting than others. The therapist may find it necessary to cultivate the art of composing blandly innocuous notes in order to resist being drawn into activities that are injurious to treatment.

The recording of private and sensitive information is related to the equally thorny question of verbally sharing information with team members. Perhaps the most useful strategy is to help co-workers learn to better understand and deal more comfortably with their own interactions with patients. In this manner, they become more skillful participants in the milieu, far less dependent on information drawn from the privacy of therapy sessions. As noted in Chapter 4, the potential of team members to participate in this manner is quite impressive. In a well-functioning milieu, the therapist can serve as a kind of consultant, helping co-workers struggle productively with the live tensions they bring from their experiences on the ward.

Confidentiality and the Bureaucracy

In the state system, hospital administrators were sometimes required by higher-ups to implement programs and procedures that were injurious to confidentiality. Their response was often governed more by bureaucratic than by clinical considerations. The devaluation inherent in the failure to protect privileged information was seldom recognized in these situations.

A directive from the state Department of Mental Health instructed hospital administrators to participate in a research project designed to identify the needs of elderly patients. The research instrument consisted of three pages of detailed questions about patients and their families. Much of the information was of an intimate and confidential nature, requiring data gathered in therapy and social work interviews. Each patient was identified by name on the questionnaire and no provision was made for obtaining their consent or the consent of family members.

At MPC, administrators informed the staff of their intention to commence with the research project without prior consultation. The announcement met with a storm of uncharacteristically vocal opposition. Many staff members objected to the study's invasiveness and lack of provision for informed consent, but this concern was rejected out of hand by administrators. Since the Department of Mental Health was the hospital's governing authority, all clinical information was at its disposal.

Administrators were unwilling to explore ways of dealing with the department's directive in a manner consistent with ethical and clinical considerations, and they refused to acknowledge any inherent right of clinicians or patients to limit access to private information. Since patients were under the hospital's care, it was the hospital's obligation to do whatever it deemed necessary to enhance their welfare. In short, administrators identified completely with the perspective of the bureaucracy.

This incident is particularly instructive because it presented hospital bureaucrats with a relatively risk-free opportunity to support clinical priorities. The Department of Mental Health directive was so blatantly in violation of accepted ethical standards that it could not have been enforced. Administrators needed only to have explained to state authorities how the system was being placed in an untenable position.

The state in fact withdrew the questionnaire before it was implemented. In terms of the present discussion, it should be noted that the required information could have been effectively communicated in the form of group statistics; there was absolutely no need to transmit data on individual cases. In addition, the assumption that elderly patients and their families would have refused to furnish properly safeguarded information—had they been asked—was entirely gratuitous.

This incident illustrates the reflexive manner in which mental health bureaucracies generate dehumanizing measures. Violations of human dignity become so routinized and self-perpetuating as to be almost invisible. After a time, it may be considered disruptive and challenging to ask if a pressing need for the measure exists or if less aggressive alternatives are available. Interpersonal and institutional pressures on the clinician and other staff members to function, in effect, as lower echelon bureaucrats are immense. The impact of enactments intensified by these pressures can be seen in almost every area of the milieu's daily functioning.

Administrators at MPC usually blamed external regulating bodies for the uncontrolled growth of bureaucratic structures or pointed to the staff's failure to respond adequately to mandates as justification for additional regulations. The staff, for its part, blamed administrators. Mutual externalization of responsibility clouded perceptions at all levels within the hospital.

Blaming and externalization made it possible to avoid confronting the ethical dilemma. While the hospital was indeed subject to a wide variety of pressures over which it had only partial control, it was also true that its response was at best weak and ambivalent. Administrators attempted to persuade the staff that they were fighting against insurmountable pressures. The reality was that many identified with the regulatory mentality and were its willing agents, voicing therapeutic platitudes while vying with one another to extend intrusive regulations. In my eleven years on the wards at MPC, there was never a concerted effort to study the clinical impact of regulatory practices or to formulate a principled and innovative response to the challenges posed by bureaucratization.

The descending spiral of regulatory control grew into a massive intrusion into the staff's ability to perform its clinical functions. The radical nature of this transformation—in which highly trained professionals were increasingly expected to conduct themselves as mindless paper shufflers—was seldom acknowledged. Habits of speech continued to reflect traditional notions of professional responsibility and clinical judgment. The staff could take note of pervasive monitoring or auditing structures, of quality control committees, and of the hospital's disciplinary apparatus. However, few recognized this complicated system as an instrumentality of surveillance and intimidation.

What is being portrayed here is a clinical setting in which massive denial had become an essential element of maintaining professional self-esteem. Clinicians and administrators had largely succeeded in persuading themselves that the hospital's mission was not radically undermined by everyday actions in the service of bureaucratic values. This was the hospital's guilty secret and a central fact of its existence.

For clinical staff, the consequences of participating in a compromised setting are immense. Attempting to cope with the sense of futility engendered by the unrelenting attacks of primitive patients on one's sense of personal worth and professional competence is difficult even in a supportive setting. These feelings become almost impossible to deal with when integrity has been eroded by participation in compromised practices. The added measure of guilt and anger may be warded off by increased cynicism, hopelessness, vengeful counterattacks, psychogenic blindness, and further retreat into ritualistic bureaucratic modes of omnipotent control and devaluation.

Clinical Supervision

Bureaucratic intrusions are typically portrayed as necessary protective measures. The implication is that clinical processes are insufficient and untrustworthy, exposing patients to abuse or inadequate care. However, the net effect of bureaucratization is to weaken certain protective structures.

Traditionally, psychiatry, psychology, and social work have placed great emphasis on the process of case supervision as a primary means of teaching clinical skills and of providing practitioners with assistance with difficult or unusual cases. Among psychotherapists, periodic or as-needed case consultations with more experienced clinicians may be a more or less permanent component of professional practice. Supervision enhances understanding of psychotherapy through an in-depth and comprehensive focus on its many dimensions. It provides protective oversight within the framework of an educational and supportive relationship with a senior practitioner, and does not usually rely on legalistic and punitive measures to teach or enforce acceptable standards of practice.

Clinical supervision is not an arcane or haphazard undertaking; it is supported by a well-established body of knowledge and experience. In the hospital setting, skilled supervisors can frequently illuminate events on the ward in a manner that is simply inaccessible to functionaries reviewing charts or interrogating suspected wrongdoers. When permitted to do so, supervision can contribute more to the growth and maintenance of safe and effective clinical services than the most grandiose of regulatory schemes.

Perhaps not surprisingly, clinical supervisors are expected to function as monitors and enforcers of the regulatory process in bureaucratized settings. In some hospitals, the functions of clinical and administrative supervision are essentially merged. Supervisors become part of the disciplinary apparatus and mete out threats and punishments. They may also be expected to serve as conduits for confidential information. Under these circumstances, supervision becomes a sterile exercise, where only the most harmless of topics are brought for discussion and where the need for self-protection and defensive justification is uppermost.

Perhaps the most crucial function of clinical supervision is providing assistance with countertransference tensions. Therapists who work with deeply disturbed patients need solidarity, trust, and support from co-workers, colleagues, and administrative personnel. Secure and effective clinical supervision is at the heart of this support system. To the extent that supervisors function as extensions of the bureaucracy, they tend to view countertransference manifestations as infractions to be controlled or punished. This stance deprives therapists of sorely needed help and leaves patients much more exposed to the vicissitudes of enactment.

7

Collective Countertransference and Parallel Process

Peter L. Giovacchini, M.D.

All the chapters of this book deal with the complex and frequently painful reactions between a hospital staff and its patients. The author stresses how tension and excitement are created in the ward setting that more often than not result in neglect and aggravation of the patients' psychopathology and the professional degradation of the staff. Everyone is vulnerable to injury, and the final state is a chaotic degeneration of the therapeutic setting.

In fact, there is often little or no concept of a therapeutic setting. The staff insists on a certain amount of comfort, and if this means that patients have to suppress the manifestations of their illness, that becomes standard protocol.

Psychoanalysts and other psychodynamically oriented psychotherapists have a therapeutic perspective and are very much concerned about creating a good treatment setting that includes, especially when treating primitively fixated patients, a holding environment (Giovacchini 1993, Winnicott 1955). Nevertheless, there are many occasions when these clinicians lose their therapeutic orientation, and in many ways behave similarly to the hospital personnel described in this book. Something happens in the therapist–patient interaction that creates serious problems for both. This is where countertransference enters the picture.

The treatment of severely disturbed patients can be arduous. It can bring out the best and the worst in us. The effects of countertransference reactions can be considered in a similar light. They can represent turning points in therapeutic relationships or they can spell total disaster.

In the past, I have divided countertransference reactions into two categories, homogeneous and idiosyncratic (Giovacchini 1989). The former refers to average expectable reactions that would be experienced by most therapists when facing certain situations. The obvious extreme would be when the patient threatens the analyst's life by brandishing a weapon. Most clinicians would feel afraid. This is a realistic response. Most homogeneous countertransference reactions are responses to subtle variations of feeling threatened and vulnerable that contain a mixture of conscious and unconscious components. Idiosyncratic responses are the outcome of the analyst's specific characterological makeup, which may or may not be disruptive to the course of treatment.

I consider all emotional responses to patients to be countertransference. As is true of idiosyncratic reactions, analysts are reacting to a larger extent to their own needs rather than to patients' material and provocations. Nevertheless, idiosyncratic reactions are always responses to stimuli within the transference context, even if the reactions are minimal. Homogeneous countertransference responses are the outcome of a mixture of conscious and unconscious reactions to the patient's material, and are determined by features of the analyst's personality that are commonly found in clinicians.

PRIMITIVE MENTAL STATES AND THE
PAINFUL SELF

Severely disturbed patients have the capacity to put their internal agitation into their therapists. Indeed, this is a feature of their psychopathology in that they project disruptive feelings into external objects. This is a method that helps them maintain some degree of equilibrium. Therapists feel these patients' pain and misery because they are forced to absorb them. They may resist internalizing such agitation but they do not have the defensive apparatus to protect themselves, nor are their egos able to soothe themselves. That part of the patient's character structure that is put into the analyst is so ego-dystonic that the painful response is compounded. The analyst is, in a sense, introjecting a disruptive mental state, but the very act of internalizing is painful because it is not congruent with what is being introjected. The analyst's self-representation is resisting what patients are externalizing, but this is, in itself, an extremely unpleasant experience.

What I have just described appears to be a series of paradoxes. It is a relationship in which the self-representations of the patient and therapist are markedly different. The unique feature of this dyad is that the analyst finds it difficult not to receive the patient's projection of an agitated mental state. The therapist does not have adequate defensive capacities to protect himself. At the same time, his self-representation cannot smoothly incorporate what is being forced into it, and this is a painful experience. These therapists often feel totally helpless and, from a treatment perspective, functionally useless. The question that these paradoxes raise is this: Why does the analyst's self-representation succumb to the patient's projections when it is obviously so incompatible with what is being projected? There is a face to the self-representation that has to be explored, and this can best be done by presenting a clinical example.

Actually, two patients are involved. The first is a 19-year-old man who was jettisoned into therapy because no one could stand him. He was so disruptive in school that the authorities had to suspend him until he could gain some calm and be contained in the classroom.

He talked incessantly, acted silly, and even tried to tie his female classmates' pony tails into knots. At home, he was extremely labile. He might go into a seemingly unprovoked rage state, grab an axe and chop down a door. He was abusive to his father but he never attacked his mother. At most, he avoided her and ignored her presence.

He started therapy on a three-times-a-week basis, but he missed ninety percent of his appointments. He had several part-time jobs but he hardly ever worked the week out because he was irresponsible and unreliable. He frequently did not show up for work and when he did, he was usually late. He was also frequently drunk and high on drugs. He began sniffing cocaine and smoking crack.

He always appeared tense and was unable to sit still. He seemed to be in a constant state of agitation. He had a very short attention span and suffered from what seemed to be perpetual anxiety. He presented a picture of an attention deficit disorder. As a child he had been diagnosed with a minimal brain disorder and had been put on Ritalin, which did not help. As he kept getting worse, he was finally institutionalized in a residential treatment center.

For several months, his frenetic behavior was unabated even with a careful selection of anti-anxiety and tranquilizing drugs. On occasion it seemed that he was improving but after a day or so, he again became hyperactive and disruptive.

It was learned that the mildly stabilized state became disrupted after his mother visited him. She was observed to hug and passionately kiss him. Some of the attendants were apprehensive that they were indulging in foreplay and about to have intercourse. Of course, the attendants would have intervened, if such were the case. The patient was always disturbed after such an encounter. In fact, his agitation became extremely severe after each visit, and he sometimes went on a rampage and would have to be physically subdued. He would also make homosexual advances to other patients, which often resulted in his being beaten up. Once the staff learned about his mother's visits, she was denied visiting privileges, and the few times she was allowed to see her son, there was always someone in attendance.

After sixteen months, he was sufficiently calmed that he was discharged from the hospital and sent to live with his father, who was now separated from his mother. He continued outpatient psychotherapy with the same analyst, and managed to keep about sixty to seventy percent of his appointments. His agitation continued but with lesser intensity and he was able to hold a menial job.

This state of minimal tranquility was threatened by the mother's insistence that he return and live with her and his siblings. Both her husband's and son's therapists believed that this would be a disaster, but she persisted. She demanded to see these analysts, but they both adamantly refused to give her an appointment. From a previous state of calm, she became increasingly agitated. Finally, they suggested that she see me as a consultant, and she agreed.

When I first saw her, contrary to what I expected, she presented herself as a quiet, demure, calm person, tastefully dressed and eager to explore the dynamics of her interaction with her children and husband. I learned that she was working for an advanced degree in the field of mental health. The course of our interaction seemed to proceed in a pleasant fashion. After about twenty minutes, I was astonished by a sudden change in my emotional orientation toward her. At first, I felt tense and anxious and then I became aware of a strong urge to strangle her. This was both disconcerting and baffling because she had continued in her calm and apparently pleasant manner.

Naturally, I was intensely curious as to what had happened. Obviously something had occurred in our relationship that had upset my psychic equilibrium. I was feeling internally agitated and destructive toward her. Still, there she was, sitting in front of me, relaxed and unperturbed.

I then tried to summarize what she had revealed to me, what I had learned from her, and I realized that I had gathered very little pertinent information. For example, I knew practically nothing about her relationship with her children. I surmised that she had two schizophrenic brothers, but I could learn nothing about her early family life and the infantile environment that could produce such severe psychopathology. The description of her parents, like everything else, was unidimensional. For some reason, the paucity of information was causing me to feel extremely frustrated. The fact that she remained tranquil was, in itself, aggravating.

I became more active in my approach in order to soothe myself. Being active was a defense against feelings of passive vulnerability and I suppose, to some extent, my being confrontational was a manifestation of a mild destructive retaliatory attack. Nevertheless, I was able to extract from her, inasmuch as she volunteered practically nothing, some highly significant data. I gathered that she lived in a neat, suburban, middle-class neighborhood with rows of moderate-size homes. The exterior of her house was clean and attractive, as was confirmed by her son. He also confirmed that the interior of the house was an utter mess, a chaotic maelstrom. Cups of coffee would be laid on the couch and would soil the furniture. Garbage was left in the middle of the living room and, on occasion, rats were found in the refrigerator. She gave me these details in response to my questions, but her affect indicated that she saw nothing unusual in this description of utter disorder and filth. She was describing an alien world, but for her it seemed to be a familiar environment.

Her appearance, however, stood in marked contrast to the surroundings she described. She was, as stated, neat and clean, and her manner of speaking and vocabulary were typical of a well-bred and genteel person. I wondered what the status of her inner life was. I thought of her house with its neat exterior and the unbelievable amount of vermin and messiness of the interior. Was I witnessing her suburban exterior but reacting to the chaos inside her? Yet, she gave no indications of internal disturbances except for a somewhat schizoid detachment, a constricted outlook, and flat affects.

Perhaps she could maintain psychic stability because she was able to externalize her inner disruption. Certainly, I was feeling it and I began gaining relief when I was able to make these connections. I viewed what was happening between us as an interesting phenomenon. Still, I wondered why I had allowed myself to accept her projections. It had been an unconscious process, but the type of chaos she had described was alien to my psychic constitution. There must have been some similarities between our emotional worlds so that hers could gain entry into mine.

There are, of course, some common qualities that define the human condition. Furthermore, those of us who live fairly orderly lives might have some craving for disorder, although the manifestation of her inner turmoil held no attraction for me whatsoever. The contrast between her exterior and interior could also have had a striking impact and caused me to relax some vigilant and protective defenses.

As I further review the course of our interaction, I believe that initially I was able to relate to the surface of her psyche, manifested by her gentle, well-bred, and intelligent demeanor. This created an opening, so to speak, in which she could then project the inner aspects of her mind into unconscious segments of my psyche. This succeeded in upsetting my emotional equilibrium which, in turn, caused me to feel agitated and hostile.

I was, in a sense, dealing with an oxymoron, orderly chaos, but at first I recognized only the surface, the order and organization she presented. She discussed the chaotic elements of her life in a calm, casual fashion, as if there was nothing out of the ordinary about them. I was able to identify with her organized self, but at the same time, I had to introject the messiness and agitation that were clothed in apparent rationality. There were two faces to my self-representation, one accepting the surface aspects of the patient and the other being disrupted by inner chaos.

Something similar had happened to her son, as was learned from his therapy. One can imagine how helpless and vulnerable he must have felt. If an adult like me, with a modicum of self-preservative adaptations, could be upset by this mother, what chance did her son have, especially as an infant without or with relatively few coping mechanisms? For some reason, the mother made this son the target of her inner craziness. He was unable to contain it. As he absorbed her agitation, he acted out by being destructive and disruptive. He lost control, inasmuch as he had no defenses to deal with what was felt as a primal agitation.

I believe that his sexual overtures toward his peers represented pathetic attempts to achieve some degree of internal organization. Both erotic feelings and anger can act as organizers of disruptive agitation. Affects, in general, have a binding effect and though they, in themselves, may lead to further chaos, their initial intent is to achieve some relief from unbearable inner tension (Giovacchini 1990). However, as was true with this adolescent, they often misfire.

COUNTERTRANSFERENCE AND
FRAGMENTATION

The psychopathology I have just discussed involves the primitive end of the developmental spectrum. The treatment of patients suffering from primitive mental states involves dealing with psyches that lack cohesion and unity. As has been repeatedly stressed, these patients often use splitting and projective mechanisms. In some instances, patients have not achieved sufficient psychic synthesis so that they can use dissociative defenses and adaptations because there has to be a certain degree of organization and structure from which the patient can fragment. These patients are already fragmented and cannot use splitting defenses because they are initially in a dissociative state.

Again, the analyst's self-representation is faced with two perspectives in the process of fusing with a fragmented patient. To be empathic, therapists often incorporate their patients' psychic structure into their own, as discussed in the previous section. They also, especially with severely disturbed patients, have to see the world through the patients' eyes. To some degree, analysts have to feel how it is to live in the patients' world. That can also be painful, as is the superimposing of the patient's psychic structure onto that of the therapist. The world that supports the patient's psychic structure can be devastating to the analyst, as I experienced when I saw the mother of the acting-out adolescent.

Furthermore, it is painful for the analyst to live in the patient's world because it is a world that has caused only misery and suffering for the patient. The analyst's natural instinct is to rescue patients from their traumatic infantile world and soothe and comfort them, to give them some type of emotional gratification. Unfortunately, with many fragmented patients, this could lead to total therapeutic catastrophe. This creates a veritable countertransference problem, because therapists are trapped in a situation in which helping the patient causes harm. This is another oxymoron: destructive help.

This type of disruptive countertransference occurs during moments in which the patient has regressed. Generally, clinicians, especially when treating severely disturbed patients, can comfortably regress. Some fragmented patients, at least for large segments of their treatment, cannot achieve a reasonable state of equilibrium during regressed mental states so that analysis is not disrupted. This is usually due to countertransference difficulties. In the past twenty years, I have encountered more and more patients who have undergone severely painful regressions which, when properly handled, lead to crucial resolution, but because of the analyst's responses, the treatment situation can often collapse.

A middle-aged single man demonstrated an intense degree of ambivalence that was a manifestation of his basic fragmentation. He was constantly facing decisions he could not make, such as where he should work, live, and even if and whom he should marry.

He had a highly traumatic background in which he had been repeatedly abandoned. He was not certain whether he was an orphan or whether the people he thought of as his mother and father were his biological parents. When he was less than a year old he was sent to live with his supposed grandparents, and after several years he was transferred to another couple who might have been his parents. When they were angry and punitive, they told him he had been adopted, but he was never quite certain.

After years of treatment, on occasion he would roll off the couch onto the floor, convulsively writhing, screaming, and crying. He also moaned as if he was feeling intense pain. He babbled, and at times I could make out some words such as "mommy," "daddy," "come back," and "don't leave me."

At first, I was taken by surprise and tried to understand what was happening. I wanted to make an interpretation but I realized that I was more interested in relieving him and myself of the painful tension he had created rather than giving him insight. My natural impulse was to comfort him and to help him regain equilibrium. Later, I was able to acknowledge to myself that I was also trying to reestablish *my* equilibrium. I had absorbed much of his pain and I wanted some relief, but I could rationalize that I was acting in the best interests of treatment.

Actually, to comfort and soothe him were the worst things I could have done. It would have brought him out of the regression and it was vital for the treatment that he get in touch with the primitive parts of his psyche, those that contained the traumatic elements of the infantile environment. The pain and misery he felt were the manifestations of attempts to gain psychic coherence and synthesis. He was struggling to integrate fragmented parts of his psyche into the main psychic current, something he could not do during the course of early development because they contained so many traumatic elements. He was reliving his traumatic experiences of abandonment with me.

Initially, I resisted being a passive observer as he returned to the infantile world. His ego state clashed with mine and this was a traumatic experience for me. He taught me that we both had to tolerate it so that it could be processed.

PROJECTIVE IDENTIFICATION, COLLECTIVE COUNTERTRANSFERENCE AND PARALLEL PROCESS

Recently, introjective-projective processes have received considerable attention (see Grotstein 1981, Klein 1946, and Ogden 1982). As clinicians study the structural aspects of psychopathology, they are including projective identification more and more in their formulations. In my opinion, this process has received too much attention, but it certainly is relevant when we direct our attention to countertransference interactions.

I want to comment briefly on why I believe that projective identification as a separate process has been overemphasized. It is a ubiquitous phenomenon that operates with varying degrees of intensity. Inherent in every sensory impression are elements of projective identification. The sensory apparatus is part of the self representation and bears its imprint. We do not hear, see, or form any impression in a purely objective manner. Our perceptions are colored by our general characterological orientation and contain our biases. In other words, a part of our personality is projected into every percept as it undergoes the process of being internalized. Freud (1925) may have meant something similar when he wrote about preconscious feelers reaching out to meet the incoming stimulus halfway.

Regarding the interactions between the representations of external objects and the self, Klein (1946) was describing a similar movement. She was referring, however, to large segments of the self moving into the container object and then once again being internalized. But basically, she was also dealing with perceptions, because the persons involved experienced feelings, distressing or otherwise, that referred to their sense of being and how they perceived themselves and others.

If the character structure of the adult is in tune with the current milieu, in that its *modus operandi,* adaptive mechanisms, and modes of relating are in harmony with the exigencies of reality, the projective aspect of projective identification is more or less silent. Clinicians view such persons as having good reality testing. Their sensory systems are in synchrony with how the world is generally perceived, so their perceptions and judgment are acceptable and usually do not contain idiosyncratic elements related to peculiar personality traits.

I have already discussed how introjective mechanisms may cause the therapist to internalized the patient's inner chaos and experience countertransference difficulties that are the outcome of increased vulnerability. Patients often interact on the basis of projective identification by projecting chaos into the analyst, who, in turn, attempts to organize what is internalized, and then the patient, by projecting what has been projected, gains much calm. The analyst, however, feels disrupted and, at times, is no longer able to function as a therapist. This can happen, regardless of the therapist's personal orientation, especially when treating primitively fixated patients.

When there are similarities in the psychopathological configurations of patient and therapist, countertransference prob-

then protectively take care of him. The seminar members surmised that the son was succumbing to the mother's projections when he was first brought to therapy. In treatment he was able to construct and discover a true self apart from the mother's projections that had threated to stifle his budding sense of autonomy. The treatment experience was so totally integrated into his self-representation and adaptations that it lost the discrete qualities of a memory. It had become incorporated in the same way as a reflex action such as breathing or an automatized coordination such as walking. It had become part of him and not simply a registration in the memory system.

The mother, on the other hand, could not allow herself to recognize how much her son had grown, especially away from her. She needed to see him as helpless and damaged and she had somehow managed to find an analyst who must have had similar needs. Patient and therapist supported each other with the illusion that their children were damaged instead of themselves. This represented a transference–countertransference collusion and the manifestations of the parallel process, that is, the similarities between patient and therapist, were truly remarkable.

They were even more remarkable when I learned about the course of treatment of the analyst's son, which was revealed to me privately. Similar to my adolescent patient, he began treatment with an intensely negative impression of himself. He felt inadequate academically, socially, and physically.

To summarize drastically, he discovered that he had an innate talent for computers and mathematics. Throughout the course of treatment, he continued working on what might be called reconstructing the self-representation. He felt the impact of his mother's projections within the transference setting and was able to struggle against their constricting effects. The task was aided by his beginning achievements in school, which extended to the social arena.

He was developing a professional identity, that of a computer scientist. He gained the admiration of both his peers and teachers and was viewed as destined to have a distinguished career. Like my patient, he was given a highly coveted scholarship.

The similarities continue. As was also true of my patient, this young man's mother vehemently opposed her son's leaving home. In her opinion, he could not survive being away; he was too weak, shy, and inhibited. She maintained that he could not possibly compete against the best student minds in the country, whereas his teachers believed in his abilities and constantly encouraged him. His analyst did not particularly want to lose his patient, but he believed that in the interest of autonomy the patient should be allowed to pursue his career.

I felt the same way about my patient and evenually, the other analyst and I succeeded in persuading these mothers that they should not interfere with their sons' endeavors. It was, however, an especially difficult task for me because the mother of my patient was supported by her analyst who, in turn, had to directly oppose her son's analyst.

The members of the seminar became quite inflamed and bitterly attacked the analyst for colluding with her patient rather than analyzing her. It was embarrassing to witness the intensity of their reaction. They were relentless to the point of cruelty. I was surprised that this mature group of experienced psychoanalysts could not feel some compassion based on understanding and insight. True, the analyst who was being attacked presented her viewpoints in a rigid and irritating fashion, but the seminar's purpose was to promote learning and to share our clinical experiences rather than to be peremptory and judgmental. In any case, the woman analyst left the group with bad feelings.

Clearly, the account of the treatment we heard represented a travesty of analysis. The psychopathology of therapist and patient dovetailed, and each encouraged the other to continue projecting destructive feelings and self-devaluations into their sons. This is an example of what I call *idiosyncratic countertransference,* since it is based on certain unique qualities and peculiarities inherent in the analyst. Her psychopathology stood in the way of treatment, and she should not have taken the patient in analysis until she resolved her own similar problems. Still, because of her problems, she was not able to make an objective evaluation and recognize her own needs.

On the other hand, the members of the seminar did not exactly represent an exemplary model. They seemed to understand the problem, but the effect generated went beyond the confines of either reason or decency. It is difficult to ascertain what the *collective countertransference* consisted of, but a certain amount of speculation is possible and may have some relevance to the encounters described in this book in the hospital setting.

I recalled other presentations in this seminar that caused me to to feel critical. My discomfort stemmed from another group member's managerial and confrontational attitude (see Giovacchini 1993). This analyst, quite the opposite of what has been described, questioned another adolescent patient's decision to remain in treatment rather than go to a famous eastern college. She attacked the therapist for not letting the patient do what was "best for him," failing to recognize that the analysand valued the treatment and was making important strides in discovering his true self, as Winnicott (1960a) would have stated. Nevertheless, many of the group members also felt that this boy should leave treatment and go to an Ivy League college. It seemed to me as if these therapists were more interested in a surface adjustment and prestige rather than developmental progression. I also wondered how ambitious they might be about their teen-aged children since many of them spent considerable time, at social occasions, talking about their scholastic and athletic achievements and their high S.A.T. scores. Again, antithetical to the first patient discussed, these parents might have been using their children to aggrandize themselves instead of as a repository for their inadequacies. Nevertheless, their attitudes may not be particularly different from what was formulated for her and my patient. Many members of the group were using their children to maintain and elevate their self-esteem. Most of these therapists came from large, low-income families, some even approaching poverty.

Although the group consisted of fully trained psychoanalysts, they seemed to have lost the intrapsychic focus on these occasions and concentrated on behavioral management. Perhaps, as a reaction formation, they were merciless in their responses to the case presentation. They may have been reacting to their own propensities to share their neuroses with their patients or children and their tendencies to manipulate a patient's behavior to elevate their self-esteem. Their condemnation can be viewed as a collective countertransference, one that may be more common in psychotherapists than we suspect, and is manifested in parallel psychic processes in the therapist and patient. Yorke (1992) has explored parallel processes in patients, therapists, and supervisors.

Unlike the situations described in the first section of this chapter, the self-representations of therapist and patient were similar and it was easy for a fusion to occur. In these transference–countertransference interactions, the participants strive toward fusion rather than resist it, as I did when interviewing the mother of an adolescent patient. In one instance the fit was too good and in the other it was too painful. Thus, on the surface, it appears that there is a comfortable and harmonious treatment relationship and neither the patient nor the therapist is aware that there are problems in the therapeutic interaction. In most instances, there is eventually a breakdown of the relationship because what is, in effect, a mutual delusion or, at best, an illusion, cannot be a long-lasting, sustaining factor and there is no treatment progression. The most quiet outcome is interminable stagnation.

The seminar group's collective countertransference has its counterparts and parallels in many of the impasses experienced on psychiatric wards. Rather than quiet stagnation, clinicians more often face disruptive encounters and confrontations, as has been repeatedly demonstrated throughout this book. I believe we can combine the two examples that were discussed in the seminar group, that of the woman analyst and her social worker patient, and the group's reaction toward that analyst, and note how similar processes underlie many of the ward dilemmas described.

The essence of the problems just discussed was the loss of the intrapsychic focus and psychic determinism. Many psychiatric wards openly acknowledge that they are not interested in the psychodynamic approach or in understanding the patient in terms of internal mental processes. The staff is interested in maintaining the peace. Disturbed patients are supposed to keep their disturbances to themselves and not inflict them on the staff. It is understandable to strive for behavioral control from the staff's viewpoint, but is such an achievement always in the best interest of the patient?

Under these circumstances, there is no treatment of emotional illness, only regimentation and modulation of behavior. As can be gathered from this book, many wards are nothing more than disciplining institutions and prisons. There is no possibility for developmental growth, nor does anyone care. What is especially sad and poignant is that there is no hope for the staff either. The richness of an experience of mental growth that occurs with a successful and humanistic psychotherapeutic approach passes them by. In dehumanizing patients, they have dehumanized themselves.

I have speculated that the members of the seminar were somewhat dissatisfied with themselves and they took it out on the presenter. I believe that basically they were disturbed with their tendency to stray from the intrapsychic perspective, that they were having conflict and feeling guilty about their professional self-representation and ego-ideal. Thus, it was easy to pounce on the victim, who was openly displaying a lack of therapeutic sensitivity, a sensitivity that many members of the group feared they too lacked.

A similar dissatisfaction occurs with many ward staffs that are seemingly unconcerned with unconscious motivations and the inner lives of their patients. Like the seminar group, they develop a collective countertransference in which patients are both targets and victims. The ward personnel's feelings of inadequacy and guilt determine the nature of their countertransference feelings, although its substance will vary according to their character structure and the patients' psychopathology. In many instances, I am postulating that staff members feel insecure regarding their professional identity and orientation. Often, they view themselves as second-class citizens and unconsciously feel that their work with patients is inferior to that of other professionals. Their problems are compounded by an intrinsic hierarchy, each level disdaining the one beneath it.

The staff faces a dilemma. They have rejected the mind, so to speak, but this leads to lowered self-esteem because their rejection is defensive and not based on an expression of the true self. Those who disdain to recognize mental processes are usually being defensive, although they may relate successfully to the external world. On a psychiatric ward, a nonpsychologically oriented staff does not have the adequate adaptive techniques to treat its patients with the goal of resolving fundamental issues. Therefore, staff members only relate to a part person and, in turn, they view themselves as professionally fragmented.

Having abandoned the psychodynamic orientation, the staff attempts to retrieve pride and prestige by adopting the medical model, a model that has commanded respect. The physician is at the top of the totem pole and psychiatrists, especially, want to practice in such a manner that they can consider themselves to be "real doctors." Because they feel threatened by intrapsychic conflict, they deny that it exists by excluding it from consideration. They do not want to know what is going on within the patient's mind; they are simply interested, at best, in symptomatic relief or, at worst, in suppressing any type of annoying activity in the patient's behavior. This is done in the proper medical tradition by

prescribing drugs. Inasmuch as there is little or no psychological perspective, the staff is unaware of its countertransference
problems, but they are not dormant; their effects are evident.

Sometimes, countertransference problems are the outcome of rivalry among different groups of staff members, as has
been described in some of the chapters of this book. I wish to
emphasize how the cutting off of narcissistic supplies designed
to reinforce the professional ego-ideal may lead to deleterious
countertransference responses. This was a factor that caused
disruption in the seminar group, but it can also happen on the
ward.

The interplay of psychopathological constellations is a
prominent feature in individual psychotherapy as well as hospital psychiatry. To repeat, sometimes the therapists on the
ward staff collude with and accept the patient's projections,
and on other occasions, they resist what the patient is trying to
intrude into them.

In some instances, both occur. For example, a hospitalized
elderly woman suffered from a severe depression. Most of the
time she sat on a chair, staring into empty space. During the
holidays, the staff and patients gave a party in the recreation
room, and the noise level was fairly high as most people were
having a good time. This patient, however, was in the hall,
standing alone and looking pathetically dejected.

The ward chief walked by and, feeling compassion for her,
put his arm around her shoulder and gently said, "Come on,
grandmother, let's join the party. You won't spoil anyone's
fun." Then he led her into the recreation room. The staff
enthusiastically greeted her, presumably to make her feel welcome, but in a few minutes, the mood of the party changed.
There was no more laughter, jollity, or merriment. She had, in
fact, spoiled their fun.

The patient felt guilty and afraid of destroying good
feelings, an essential feature of her depression. She isolated
herself to protect others from herself. The staff, apparently,
had accepted her projections, which destroyed their gaiety.

This was a psychodynamically oriented ward, so during a staff conference, their consultant was able to point out what had happened. Everyone felt enlightened and sympathetic toward the patient, whereas previously they had felt resentment toward her without knowing why.

In summary, to deny a patient's psychic life is a dehumanizing experience for both the patient and the therapist. It is tantamount to extracting life forces and turning the person into a robot that is supposed to respond predictably. A certain dosage of a particular drug will have specific effects, as will certain ward routines and rules and regulations. There is no human interaction, just a reflex-like connection. The therapist, because he is also barring his inner psychic world, may feel protected. He is unaware of his countertransference responses, but, nevertheless, he feels unconsciously demeaned. This causes him to become, as a reaction formation, even more antagonistic to psychic phenomena.

THE USELESS THERAPIST

I have just discussed therapists and ward staff who have taken the life out of the treatment situation and have adopted a mechanistic medical model that leads to the formation of unrecognized countertransference problems. There are clinical interactions, however, in which the analyst has a very well-developed intrapsychic focus, but the patient, because of a concrete orientation and special characterological problems, will not allow the analyst to function within a psychodynamic framework. This leads to severe countertransference impasses.

Life, or the experience of living, is very difficult for these patients. Flarsheim (1975) described a patient who was reputed to be a fussy baby. Her parents hired a nurse who had a reputation for being an expert in handling such babies. Her method was simple and expeditious. Whenever the child indicated a need, she would immediately respond but not to the need. If the baby was hungry, she would change her diaper, and if the baby was wet, she would feed her. Furthermore, she put some sort of gloves on the baby's hands that made it impossible for the infant to suck her thumb. She made it impossible for the child to receive either gratification or soothing.

As she grew up, the world seemed inordinately complex. She did not know how to relate at most levels. Socially she was isolated to the degree of being considered autistic. She could not articulate her needs and her outlook lacked all vibrancy; she presented a picture of deadness that some interpreted as depression.

Such patients in therapy present a highly concrete outlook because there is a poorly developed sense of aliveness. At first, the experience of aliveness is the outcome of needs. Babies have needs; they are nurtured and soothed and the ensuing comfort is associated with a vital equilibrium. The child can then move into the world, explore it with pleasure and rudimentary anticipation. This is the beginning of a life feeling based on the security that inner needs will be gratified and that the external world is in resonance with them.

The patients I have been describing find their needs painful, so the life process is experienced as a traumatic event. They are not at all in resonance with their milieu. The external world is a strange, alien, and threatening place and they are psychologically dead.

Some patients need a therapist with a similar characterological constellation, as discussed in the previous section. They are unable to accept a therapist who has a vibrant sense of aliveness because they experience such feelings as painful and they are unable to integrate them. In such instances, the patient attempts to make the analyst useless, which is better than perceiving him as assaultive and dangerous. That is how Flarsheim's patient viewed the nurse or any other person who attempted to assume a caregiving role.

Another patient, a single woman in her middle thirties, had never left her parental home. Her childhood was similar to that of the patient just discussed. Her father sexually and physically abused her and her mother was described as withdrawn, fearful, and incompetent, unable to nurture or protect her daughter effectively. She did not abuse the patient as did the father; she was simply incompetent and inadequate to the task of raising a child. The patient had no assurance that her needs would be taken care of. In fact, she was not even able to recognize them. She literally did not know whether she was hungry, thirsty, had to move her bowels, or urinate. She was just aware of vague abdominal and chest sensations and "experimentally" reacted to them. She had many of the features of an alexithymic patient.

The patient lived with her mother. Her father, an alcoholic, was killed in an auto accident, apparently drunk at the time. The patient devoted her life to taking care of her mother, who was becoming increasingly infirm, and never had any close friends or heterosexual relationships.

It is not entirely clear why she sought therapy, but her mother was quite old and weak and the patient feared the mother might die. Obviously there was some type of symbiotic relationship between the two which, in some way, maintained them.

During the first interview, the patient presented herself in a flat, dead fashion. All she could say about her reasons for seeking treatment was that she was unhappy with life and could not or would not elaborate further. She apologized several times for being uncooperative and not more revealing. She gave the therapist her telephone number, but did not want him to call because she did not want her mother to know that she was in treatment. The analyst was not particularly sanguine about a patient who did not want to talk about herself and who could not be reached.

He was somewhat heartened when she told him she had read Freud and he was surprised that she had some knowledge of psychoanalysis. His spirits once again dropped when she stated she did not want to get involved in a psychoanalytic exchange and she would have "nothing to do with transference." Nevertheless, they set up a four-times-a-week treatment schedule on a face-to-face basis because clearly she would not tolerate lying down on the couch.

After eighteen months of treatment, a duration that had never been anticipated, the therapist came to me for supervision because he felt thoroughly frustrated. He felt the patient had been true to her word and never formed a transference except perhaps for the first few weeks of therapy, when she was pleased with her interviews and looked forward to them. After that it had been strictly downhill.

Though the patient denied being depressed, she emphasized how dissatisfied she was with her treatment. The therapist, who ordinarily had a cheerful and bright outlook, felt depressed. He described his office as suffused with deadness and as having the aura of a funeral parlor.

The patient claimed she never understood anything he told her, so he was not being helpful. He reported that she never rejected an interpretation or argued with him to prove him wrong. She simply would exasperatedly state that she did not know what he was talking about, as if he were speaking in a foreign language. Consequently she not only blamed him for the lack of improvement, but because of his ineptness, her condition was rapidly deteriorating.

The analyst experienced the relationship with his patient as if she were a bulldog clamped on his clothes and relentlessly hanging on, or as if he were being constantly pounded with a baseball bat. The therapist described himself as being numb with all of his vitality crushed. He frequently had headaches and suffered from many aches and pains, a cursious phenomenon because otherwise he was seldom if ever ill. He explained his frustration as being due to her total lack of an intrapsychic focus and his lack of ability to treat her.

He presented himself to me as professionally incompetent. His disturbing countertransference reactions stemmed from his incapacity to treat her. She made him feel totally useless. She had also made inroads into his professional ego-ideal, disrupting his psychic equilibrium and making him further incapable of conducting what he considered to be adequate treatment.

Though the patient was concretely oriented and lacked an intrapsychic focus, she certainly was involved in a transference struggle. She may have wanted "nothing to do with transference" but had dominated the consultation room with her transference projections, which had created a countertransference that had almost totally disrupted her therapist, something she had never succeeded in doing with her mother. The patient was getting revenge on her inept, unprotective mother by making the therapist incompetent and then attacking him. She was displacing her mother's ineptness onto him. Furthermore, she was also reversing the relationship with her father. Whereas her father abused her, she was now bitterly attacking the therapist, causing him to feel even more helpless, vulnerable, and inadequate.

The therapist was unable to accept the patient's projections because he did not understand them and they were not in resonance with his character structure. The patient could modulate painful feelings stemming from what was essentially privation, as discussed by Winnicott (1963), by covering them with feelings of deadness, and she suffused the consultation room with such feelings. This was also extremely painful for the analyst because he could not abide by the oxymoron dead aliveness, as could the patient. She had made this oxymoron the central theme of her existence, and she could only soothe herself in this perverse fashion, that is by deadening all feelings and smothering the sense of aliveness.

Once the analyst understood the dynamics of the treatment relationship and the existence of transference projections, he felt somewhat relieved. Though the patient's attitude was strictly concrete and devoid of any intrapsychic focus, something, nevertheless, of psychological significance was going on. He was able to relax with his patient and kept pointing out the patient's need to devalue the treatment, because she herself had never been valued, cherished, or protected. Gradually, the patient softened and after a year of further treatment, she began to understand that the analyst valued her and the treatment relationship. The treatment relationship was able to establish a holding environment and the patient reached a state of comfortable dependency. In my mind, this is a considerable achievement. The treatment continues, and I suspect it will go on for many years.

This was an example in which countertransference problems were created because of differences in the character structure of the patient and the therapist. Of course, such differences should and usually do exist, and, it is hoped, there is a differential between patient and analyst so that therapy can be effective (see Loewald 1960). The analyst's higher level of differentiation enables him to help the patient achieve a more integrated structural level.

In this instance, the patient had to bring the analyst down to her more primitive level and make him relate to her within the context of infantile traumas. To some extent, this regularly occurs in psychoanalytic treatment and the transference is organized around the repetition compulsion (Freud 1920). Because of the patient's lack of psychological orientation, her analyst was unable to view their relationship from an intrapsychic focus. She had restricted her therapist's viewpoint to surface phenomena because that is where she was in her discourse, and he was unable to get in touch with internal processes.

The therapist felt the treatment was going nowhere, and the patient not only stimulated that attitude but constantly intensified it. The therapist despaired because he felt that he lacked the therapeutic technique to deal with this type of patient. What he had failed to see was that, in a sense, what had happened *should* have happened. The patient needed to view him as useless and dead, two qualities his professional ego-ideal vehemently rejected. Once he understood that he was witnessing an inevitable course of treatment, his internal psychic equilibrium was restored and he became much more receptive. What had been a countertransference impasse led to insight and the construction of a more comfortable analytic relationship.

MUTUAL DEPENDENCE AND DEADNESS

In another treatment relationship, the outcome was not quite as felicitous with the first therapist but the second analysis went well. The patient, again a middle-aged woman, had conflict about letting a sense of autonomy emerge. She was a "pseudo as-if" character, as Deutsch (1942) described. To feel separate caused anxiety. This was especially true in her relationship with her husband.

There was considerable evidence to support the formulation that autonomy was threatening. She recalled the words of a song that her mother had sung to her while feeding her. The mother's tone was tender, but the words referred to the abandonment and death of a baby. This was a dominant memory, and perhaps was a significant indicator of the atmosphere of the nurturing relationship and the infantile milieu. In any case, to be alive and autonomous, the two being equated, was perceived as threatening and she protected herself by fusing with those involved in an emotionally meaningful relationship.

Her second therapist could formulate what occurred in her first analysis as the treatment relationship progressed. She reported many dreams indicating that she had fused with her analyst and felt totally attached to him. In her fantasies she was connected to him with an umbilical "soul" substance that lengthened as she moved away from him. She always wanted to feel tied to him.

This analyst was a depressed personality and it seemed dubious whether he was consicously aware of any fusion. He never made any interpretations or comments about it, but he had recognized the patient's pseudo as-if character. Perhaps he thought of her as an as-if personality, the same way the patient had viewed herself. I surmised that both patient and therapist found the sense of aliveness painful and they received relief in a fusion of deadness.

This conclusion was reinforced by a fantasy the patient and analyst shared. Her therapist told her that psychoanalysis was dead and the only way for it to survive was to put it in a display case in a museum; he as a psychoanalyst should be stuffed by a taxidermist and put on exhibit, whereupon the patient replied that there is no such thing as a psychoanalyst without a patient, so she should also be stuffed, put on a couch, and placed in the same display case beside him. Thus, survival was dependent on deadness.

I believe that here again we have an example of a stale-mated therapy because the psychopathology of participants was remarkably similar. In this instance, the analyst needed the patient in order to maintain himself. He was not aware of any countertransference feelings, but it was obvious that he was highly dependent upon patients who lived in a dead world.

Because of fortuitous circumstances, the therapy had to be discontinued, and the patient sought treatment with another analyst. The second analyst was a vibrant type who in no way enjoyed or needed an aura of deadness. The patient was able to form a bond with him, not necessarily a fusion, because she was gradually able to develop and enjoy a sense of autonomy that was experienced as an awakening. Recently she had a dream in which she was in her first analyst's office. There was a young, retarded woman there who was mute and did not express any feelings. The first analyst was also mute. The current analyst equated being mute with deadness and the patient agreed. Her analyst also interpreted that she was dreaming of herself as she was, that is, a dead non-person, during the first therapy. She was trying to show him how different she was now. The patient added that nothing was happening in the office. The retarded girl was simply sitting there, apparently devoid of feelings. From her present analyst's viewpoint, it was a dead room and he was reminded of the display case in the museum. The patient commented that they were all involved in a stalemate. It was a stymied situation, an impasse.

At first, the patient was dismayed by this dream, believing it was a "bad" dream. She was delighted with the intepretation and complimented her therapist on his ability to extract the positive and adaptive attributes of her material, whereas her previous analyst had cast everything in a morbid and depressive tone. She felt that the interpretation clicked and stated that there was more to the dream that confirmed it. She added that she left the consultation room to buy a cup of black coffee. She saw this as acting on her own, an experience that was equated with awakening. Black coffee is strong, and she knew that her first therapist always drank weak coffee with considerable cream. She now felt that she was awakening to life, finding many experiences pleasant as she continued to establish her boundaries. In the dream, moving into the external world to get a cup of coffee was also an allusion to her second therapy. This therapist frequently drinks black coffee during her sessions, and she equated the coffee with vitality.

Parenthetically, her husband's reactions were interesting. He was extremely supportive of the first therapy but he objected to the second analysis, particularly the frequency of sessions. He had a need for his wife to be subservient and to haver her fuse with him. The patient elaborated that they were both stuck and her first analyst knew it, but she found it difficult to leave him. On one occasion she was able to leave treatment, but she felt badly because she had to come back. He reassured her that it was proper that she returned because she needed maintenance. He also commented about the mutual needs of patient and analyst, which seemed to indicate that he also needed maintenance. In his usual depressed fashion, he stated that the only reason for her to leave treatment would be that she would not have to mourn him when he died. He felt threatened at the prospect of her separating from him, as she was, in fact, doing, in a psychic sense.

This patient's mode of relating involved fusing with emotionally significant persons. Many years ago (Giovacchini 1958), I wrote about stable, but not necessarily comfortable, marital relationships being the outcome of a symbiotic merger. Recently much has been written about co-dependence, which I believe is a new word for an old concept, that of symbiosis. I had postulated, however, that symbiosis in the psychic realm meant that the persons involved in such a merger had a similar character structure and if there was significant psychopathology, that, too, would be similar.

In other words, hysterics marry hysterics, schizophrenics marry schizophrenics, and, as my data indicated, alcoholics marry alcoholics. There is a mutual dependence based on identical characterological configurations.

In many instances, the relationship is based on complementariness. For example, the spouse of an actively drinking alcoholic may be a self-righteous teetotaler. If the husband, however, gives up drinking, as may occur with a successful analysis, the wife often starts drinking, indicating that she is a latent alcoholic. This is not an infrequent occurrence with the spouses of alcoholics, especially those who have controlled their drinking, perhaps through the help of A.A.

Analysts are familiar with the resistances of spouses, other family members, and even close friends, to the treatment when patients make significant advances (Giovacchini 1961). The psychic equilibrium achieved by a symbiotic relationship is disturbed when the patient no longer has the same needs. This often creates a crisis that in a marriage may lead to a divorce, or, hopefully, the partner seeks treatment for himself. In some instances, the partner may go through further psychic development without treatment and reestablish a higher level equilibrium.

As discussed, this type of symbiosis can occur in psychoanalytic treatment. There is a parallel process between patient and analyst that leads to mutual dependence and fusion. In many instances, the painful feelings of aliveness are numbed by deadness, and this occurs in a symbiotic context.

Not all processes, however, result in a symbiotic fusion. I do not believe the analyst treating the social worker discussed in the seminar group was symbiotically fused. They supported each other's neurotic outlooks, but other than this collusion, they were markedly different. The dovetailing of psychopathology involved only a segment of their personalities, whereas in symbiotic relationships there is total characterological involvement. There are varying degrees of parallel process.

SUMMARY AND CONCLUSIONS

This chapter has, for the most part, examined idiosyncratic types of countertransference. Analyst's however, will absorb and react to patients' projections of internal agitation even when there are significant differences in their and the patients' emotional orientation.

The similarities, however, between the psychic structure of patient and analyst can lead to many serious therapeutic disruptions and impasses. The first example presented shed some light on group processes as well, which have implications for psychiatric ward personnel and their reactions toward patients.

One of the most painful countertransference reactions analysts can experience is being made to feel useless and incompetent. These analysts are derailed from the analytic track and often feel inadequate to the therapeutic task. What they have failed to realize is that they are caught up in the patient's transference projections and externalizations. The analyst represents the incompetent parent who has failed the child. Similarly the analyst is failing the patient, but this is an inevitable consequence of the therapeutic process. The problem is compounded when the patient externalizes the traumatic, infantile milieu into the consultation room, and then anything the therapist does is viewed as an assault.

Finally, a certain type of collusion between patient and analyst is examined in which they are locked in a symbiotic fusion. Both participants are able to obtain a modicum of psychic equilibrium, but the patient, especially, has abandoned any strivings toward individuation and autonomy. These relationships are usually dead ones in which excitement and the sense of aliveness is numbed.

There are many situations in individual therapy that resemble those occurring on psychiatric wards. There is also a parallel process between the group and the interactions of individual psychotherapy and psychoanalysis.

An awareness of subtle and hidden countertransference reactions brings us closer to our basic humanity and enlarges our therapeutic arsenal. This can be a painful experience that many therapists would like to avoid, and often do, but if we can survive it, the benefits can be incalculable for both patients and therapists.

Coda

Many psychiatric hospitals are less than adequate, sometimes distressingly so. No one knows this better than mental health professionals. Many of us feel we should have done better; that we have not is hurtful to our self-respect. In searching for explanations, we make many true observations: if only hospitals were better staffed and supported, families and communities more understanding, the medications more effective.

I have attempted here to suggest another way of thinking about these troubling circumstances. Certain of the psychiatric hospital's most characteristic failings can be viewed in the same manner that we customarily view symptoms, that is, as compromise formations conveying invaluable clinical insight into the dynamic forces operating at various organizational and psychological levels within the hospital.

Primitive patients create a remarkable world around themselves, and it is daunting to see how effectively they make use

233

of the materials at hand. To an important extent, the hospital and those of us who work in it are the materials at hand. From this perspective, the psychiatric hospital may be the setting par excellence in which to study the subjective, interpersonal, and institutional transformations and ramifications of primitive mental processes.

When hospitals fail, it is not because they are susceptible to taking on components of the primitive patient's internal world, but because they do not sufficiently make clinical use of their susceptibility. Maladaptive responses to primitive tensions can be seen as an unfortunate but potentially useful complication of the treatment process. The understanding and skills that can be gained in learning to cope with these complications may be applicable to a wide range of clinical problems encountered in and out of hospitals.

It is important to keep in mind that unconscious tensions may find their way into almost any manifest hospital procedure and transform it into a channel for enactment. Thus, carefully thought-out organizational arrangements are not a substitute for analyzed and trained clinicians. However, it is also clear that some forms of hospital organization are more likely than others to support enactment and distancing and to discourage containment and working over. I have attempted in these pages to help clinicians better recognize and understand these forms of organization.

References

American Psychiatric Association (1987). *Diagnostic and Statistical Manual of Mental Disorders* (third ed., revised). Washington, DC: American Psychiatric Association.

Bellak, L., Hurvich, M., and Gediman, H. (1973). *Ego Functions in Schizophrenics, Neurotics, and Normals.* New York: Wiley-Interscience.

Bion, W. (1967). *Second Thoughts: Selected Papers on Psychoanalysis.* New York: Basic Books.

Blanck, G., and Blanck, R. (1974). *Ego Psychology: Theory and Practice.* New York: Columbia University Press.

Boyer, L. (1979). Countertransference with severely regressed patients. In *Countertransference,* ed. L. Epstein and A. Feiner, pp. 347–374. New York: Jason Aronson.

Deutsch, H. (1942). Some forms of emotional disturbances and their relationship to schizophrenia. *Psychoanalytic Quarterly* 11:301–321.

Flarsheim, A. (1975). Therapist's collusion with the patient's wish for suicide. In *Tactics and Techniques in Psychoanalytic Therapy,* vol. 2, ed. P. Giovacchini, pp. 155–196. New York: Jason Aronson.

Freud, A. (1936). *The Ego and the Mechanisms of Defense.* New York: International Universities Press, 1966.

—— (1965). *Normality and Pathology in Childhood.* New York: International Universities Press.

Freud, S. (1910). The future prospects of psycho-analytic therapy. *Standard Edition* 11:139–152.

—— (1912). Recommendations for physicians practicing psychoanalysis. *Standard Edition* 12:109–120.

—— (1920). Beyond the pleasure principle. *Standard Edition* 18:3–66.

—— (1925). A note on the mystic writing pad. *Standard Edition* 19:227–235.

Fromm-Reichmann, F. (1950). *Principles of Intensive Psychotherapy.* Chicago: University of Chicago Press.

Giovacchini, P. (1958). Mutual adaptation in various object relationships. In *Treating Character Disorders,* pp. 179–194. Northvale, NJ: Jason Aronson, 1993.

—— (1961). Resistance and external object relationships. In *Treating Character Disorders,* pp. 194–210. Northvale, NJ: Jason Aronson, 1993.

—— (1975). *Psychoanalysis of Character Disorders.* New York: Jason Aronson.

—— (1979). Countertransference with primitive mental states. In *Countertransference,* ed. L. Epstein and A. Feiner, pp. 235–265. New York: Jason Aronson.

—— (1989). *Countertransference Triumphs and Catastrophes.* Northvale, NJ: Jason Aronson.

—— (1990). Erotism and chaos. *Journal of the Academy of Psychoanalysis* 18:186–204.

—— (1993). *Borderline States, the Psychosomatic Focus and the Therapeutic Process.* Northvale, NJ: Jason Aronson.

Giovacchini, P., and Boyer, L. (1982). *Technical Factors in the*

Treatment of the Severely Disturbed Patient. New York: Jason Aronson.

Goffman, E. (1961). *Asylums.* New York: Anchor, Doubleday.

Greenson, R. (1967). *The Technique and Practice of Psychoanalysis.* New York: International Universities Press.

Grotstein, J. (1981). *Splitting and Projective Identification.* New York: Jason Aronson.

Hartmann, H. (1958). *Ego Psychology and the Problem of Adaptation.* New York: International Universities Press.

_____ (1964). *Essays in Ego Psychology.* New York: International Universities Press.

Heimann, P. (1950). On countertransference. *International Journal of Psycho-Analysis* 31:81–84.

_____ (1955). A combination of defense mechanisms in paranoid states. In *New Directions in Psycho-Analysis,* ed. M. Klein, P. Heimann, and R. Money-Kyrle, pp. 240–265. London: Tavestock.

Kernberg, O. (1976). *Object Relations Theory and Clinical Psychoanalysis.* New York: Jason Aronson.

_____ (1980). *Internal World and External Reality.* New York: Jason Aronson.

_____ (1984). *Severe Personality Disorders.* New Haven: Yale University Press.

_____ (1987). Projective identification, countertransference, and hospital treatment. *Psychiatric Clinics of North America* 10:257–272.

Klein, M. (1946). Notes on some schizoid mechanisms. *International Journal of Psycho-Analysis* 27:99–110.

Kohut, H. (1971). *The Analysis of the Self.* New York: International Universities Press.

Langs, R. (1973). *The Technique of Psychoanalytic Psychotherapy.* New York: Jason Aronson.

Loewald, H. (1960). On the therapeutic action of psychoanalysis. *International Journal of Psycho-Analysis* 41:16–32.

Main, T. (1957). The ailment. In *Essential Papers on Object Relations,* ed. P. Buckley, pp. 419–446. New York: New York University Press, 1986.

Ogden, T. (1982). *Projective Identification and Psychotherapeutic Technique.* Northvale, NJ: Jason Aronson.

——— (1986). *The Matrix of the Mind.* Northvale, NJ: Jason Aronson.

——— (1989). *The Primitive Edge of Experience.* Northvale, NJ: Jason Aronson.

Racker, H. (1968). *Transference and Countertransference.* New York: International Universities Press.

Reich, A. (1951). On countertransference. *International Journal of Psycho-Analysis* 32:25–31.

——— (1960). Further remarks on countertransference. *International Journal of Psycho-Analysis* 41:389–395.

Rosenfeld, H. (1964). On the psychopathology of narcissism: a clinical approach. *International Journal of Psycho-Analysis* 45:332–337.

Schafer, R. (1968). *Aspects of Internalization.* New York: International Universities Press.

Searles, H. (1965). *Collected Papers on Schizophrenia and Related Subjects.* New York: International Universities Press.

Stanton, A., and Schwartz, M. (1954). *The Mental Hospital.* New York: Basic Books.

Szasz, T. (1961). *The Myth of Mental Illness.* New York: Harper and Row.

——— (1965). *The Ethics of Psychoanalysis.* New York: Basic Books.

Winnicott, D. (1945). Primitive emotional development. In *Through Paediatrics to Psycho-Analysis,* pp. 145–156. New York: Basic Books, 1975.

——— (1949). Hate in the countertransference. *International Journal of Psycho-Analysis* 30:69–75.

——— (1955). Metapsychological and clinical aspects of regression within the psycho-analytic set-up. *International Journal of Psycho-Analysis* 36:10–26.

_____ (1960). The theory of the parent–infant relationship. In *Maturational Processes and the Facilitating Environment,* pp. 37–55. New York: International Universities Press, 1965.

_____ (1960a). Ego distortions in terms of true and false self. In *The Maturational Processes and the Facilitating Environment,* pp. 140–153. New York: International Universities Press.

_____ (1963). The mentally ill in your case load. In *The Maturational Processes and the Facilitating Environment,* pp. 217–230. New York: International Universities Press.

Yorke, J. M. (1992). *Parallel Process: Treatment Implications for Psychoanalysis.* Ph.D. dissertation.

Index

Giovacchini, P., 215
  on affect, 206
  on antidepressant
    medications, 72
  on classification of character
    structure, 66
  on holding environment, 200
  on intolerable
    countertransferences, 4–5
  on learning from patient, xi
  on marital relationships, 229
  on regressive countertrans-
    ference experiences, 64
Giovacchini, P. and Boyer, L. on
    ego psychology, 143
Goals, bureaucratization and,
    187
Goffman, E. on dehumanization,
    36
Gratification and loss, 26–30
  case study, 26–28
  countertransference, anxieties
    and, 29
  limitless nurturing, demand
    for, 29
Greenson, R. on definition of
    countertransference, 1
Grotstein, J.
  on introjective–projective
    processes, 209
Group dynamics, staff meetings
    and, 48

Hartmann, H. on ego's
    executive and adaptive
    functions, 143, 144
Hatred, evocation of
  case histories, 153–155
  reality indoctrination and,
    154–155
  reciprocal psychological
    regulation and, 156

sadistic treatment
    interventions and, 156
Heimann, P.
  on communicative and
    classical counter-
    transference, 2
  on projection and
    reintrojection, 7–8
Hierarchical control,
    bureaucratization and, case
    history, 178–179
Holding environment, treatment
    milieu as, 8
  establishment of, 225
  hospital ward and, 200
Homeostasis, projective
    identifications and, 8
Homogeneous
    countertransference
    described, 398
Hospital. See also Ward
  vs. dyadic treatment, 115–116
  dynamics, 10
  practices, injurious, xiii
  procedures, continuity of care
    and, 40–42
  therapeutic setting and,
    199–200, 217

Idealization, manifestation of
    primitive omnipotence, 18
Idealized nurturer, 25–26
Identification
  complementary, definitions
    of, 3–4
  concordant, definition of, 3
  with primitive ego states, 65
  projective, 7–9
    definition of, 7
    enactment and, 7
    homeostasis and, 8